Front cover:
Gallic warrior god

Pages 2/3:
Titania Sleeping
Nymphes and elves and imps
Dadd Richard (1819 – 1867)

Pages 6/7
The Orkneys archaeological site in Scotland
Runic inscriptions probably engraved by
12ᵗʰ century Viking warriors were discovered in
this tomb in the Unstan burial mound

Back cover:
The Dream of Ossian
Jean-Dominique Ingres, about 1812

Photographic credits:

Hervé Champollion: 6/7, 30/31, 37, 46/47, 50/51, 62/63.
R. M. N.: 1, 2/3, 11, 13, 16/17, 18/19, 21, 22/23, 26/27, 29, 33,35, 38/39, 43,45, 55, 57, 58/59, 65, 66/67, 69, 72/73, 77, 78/79, 81, 85, 86/87, 104/105, 116/117, 118/119.
Tallandier archives: 14/15, 25, 60/61, 74/75.
Odette Boucher: 40, 41.
Private collection: 70/71, 76, 83, 89, 90/91, 94/95, 97, 98/99, 103, 109, 112/113, 120/125.

Text: Thierry Bordas

Contribution: F. B. S. B.

Published by Grange Books
an imprint of Grange Books Plc
The Grange
Kingsnorth Industrial Estate
Hoo, nr Rochester
Kent ME3 9ND
www.Grangebooks.co.uk
ISBN: 1-840136-901

CELTIC MYTHOLOGY

Thierry Bordas

Foreword
Pierre Brunel

Grange
BOOKS

FOREWORD

In Les Dieux antiques [The Gods of Antiquity], published in 1890, Mallarmé devoted only eight pages to what he called "Norse myths". Taking the ancient migration described by Hölderlin in his great poem of 1801, he relates these stories to Hindu and Persian myths. It is not necessary, however, to go this far back, or to summon the "Son of the Sun" from the Vedic Age. Neither do we need to limit ourselves to the so-called Nordic gloom by recognizing in these northern mythologies only the "somber and grave character" of which Mallarmé spoke. Not everything is a "Chant des enfants de la brume" [song of the children of the fog], nor does everything end with the Twilight of the Gods, on which Richard Wagner wrote his tetralogy, The Ring, in 1876, from which the French poet wrote "Crépuscule des dieux norses". [Twilight of the Norse Gods].

In this book, The Mythology of the Celts and the Vikings, Thierry Bordas clearly establishes the links between the two civilizations. Yet rather than distancing them, he manages to relate them and bring them closer to us. In a Gallic country, one cannot but sense the Celtic soul, nor in Normandy can one ignore the historic importance of the landing of the Vikings. The mythologies of the Celts and the Scandinavians are intertwined in our imagination; they are not in any way displaced by Greek or Roman mythology. Migrations of peoples have always occurred, creating mythological strata that have enriched the collective soul. Tristan and Isolde, Merlin and King Arthur are just as much part of our being as Sigurd-Siegfried, Brunhild the Valkyrie, and the mysterious ring which, like Helen before it, was the subject of a long dispute. Paul Claudel, quoting the treasures of Memory in his great Ode to the Muses, allowed us to hear the "trumpets over the Adriatic" and this "alto phrase just and strong", the "sigh of the Hercynian forest". These were for him "the original gold infused into the human substance".

"The gold, or the inner knowledge, that each thing in itself possesses, buried within the element, guarded jealously beneath the Rhine by the nixies and the Nibelungs."

A comparison on the same level would be dangerous here, and one can only admire Thierry Bordas and éditions Molière for having at once combined and distinguished Celtic and Viking mythology. Cernunnos, presented as 'the god of the stag woods" and reminiscent of the "the mysterious Dis pater", was the god of all who lived in what was originally a society of hunters. He is a multi-faceted masculine figure; although this image might disturb us today, it was definitely reassuring for those who worshipped him.

Cuchulainn was the most famous hero of Irish mythology. As a stag hunter and protector of all the inhabitants of Ulster, he was able to triumph over the giant despite the magic fog in which his adversary was hiding. In the poetry of William Butler Yeats (1865-1939), he became the symbolic figure of superhuman courage. Further, Ulli by Patrice de la Tour du Pin (1911-1975) owes something of its mystery to him. Odin, the great god of the Vikings (Wotan in the Wagner tetralogy) is the traveler, as is Ossian, the son of Finn, in one of the most powerful Fenian myths. As chief of the gods and master of magic, Odin, the "warrior wolf", also leads the Wild Hunt.

With these mythologies, we are undoubtedly far removed from the conception of Edith Sôdergran (1892-1923), the great Finnish poet of the Swedish language: here God (Gud) is not "bed of rest" for us to "stretch out upon throughout the universe", "a pillow for our head and a support for our feet". In the words of the author of the Septemberlyran [September Lyre] (1918) and of the Landet som icke är [Country that does not exist] (published posthumously 1925), he is instead a "reserve of energy" from which the heroes take their power – a source and a resource perhaps for a humanity who cannot follow at the same pace, who cannot ascend the same summits but who benefits from being carried to the top. The stones of Stonehenge should not turn us cold, Thor "The Thunderer" should not frighten us, the Norns should not divide or deliver us to the "slumbering reptile" which "straightens up hissing" as announced by the third of them in one of the Poèmes barbares [Barbarian poems] (1862) by Leconte de Lisle. These mythologies of the Celts and the Vikings still have something to say to us. This beautiful book makes it possible to understand and appreciate this.

Pierre Brunel
Professor of Comparative Literature
at the Sorbonne
Member of l'Institut Universitaire de France

CONTENTS

ï alone en celle tháßc
dist le roy or alez auãt
fait galaad de p dieu
et lorg bont dedans

Et quit ilz sont dedens si vroiet lagreusse

CELTIC MYTHOLOGY

The Celtic Peoples

Established since the end of the second millennium BC in the valley of the Danube and, without doubt, descendants of the first Indo-Europeans, the Celts occupy a special place in our collective memory. Their name first appears in the writing of Hécatée de Milet, five centuries before Christ. Their descendants in the Middle Ages were major contributors to the birth of medieval literature with courtly romances and epics, evoking ancient legends such as Tristan and Isolde or the stories of King Arthur and the Knights of the Round Table.

During the millennium before Christ, the Celts were the predominant ethnic group in Europe, both in terms of their creative force and their expansionism. Originally from Bohemia and southern Germany, they became established in most European countries spreading to Gaul, Great Britain, northern Spain, northern Italy, the Balkans, Hungary, Greece and as far as Asia Minor. They spoke the same language, although this did not necessarily imply that they shared a common culture.

Being great horsemen in the image of Epona, the goddess of travellers, or of Rhiannon (sometimes called Rhéannon), the goddess of horsemen, they travelled with their heavy four-wheeled chariots but, when conditions permitted, they settled. Even if the Celtic peoples were originally migratory tribes, they occupied vast territories over a long period, from the Atlantic to the Carpathians, establishing a civilisation of warriors, stockbreeders and merchants.

The influence of this civilisation contributed greatly to the emergence of Europe in history. Some of the first tangible evidence of this was provided by the Urnfield culture, characterised by the burial mounds constructed by the people of this period. The ashes of the dead were placed in terracotta urns arranged in vast cemeteries.

Some notable tombs of this type were uncovered in Marienburg in East Prussia. This period between 1500 to 900 BC was also marked by large-scale mining of metal deposits in places such as Mitterberg near Salzburg.

The Hallstatt culture

The Hallstatt culture, from the name of an archaeological deposit in the Austrian Salzkammergut, marks the passage of the Iron Age after 900 BC. In addition to the characteristics of the previous period – working the land, relatively dense human settlement, bronze work, the development of metallurgy – there was now also a marked increase in commercial activity. Celtic civilisation became established in Austria, eastern France and Great Britain.

The well-equipped warriors wore conical helmets sometimes decorated with horns and were armed with daggers, spears and long swords. They were protected by shields and, according to several ancient writers, such as Polybius or Diodore of Sicily, they fought naked. More often, however, they were dressed and sometimes even protected by iron coats of mail. They all wore magnificent jewellery made of gold or inlaid with silver, and sounded harsh war horns called carnyx, the sound of which drove fear into the hearts of their enemies. Bronze statuettes of warriors discovered near Balzers, Lichtenstein, or the foot soldiers represented on the Gundestrup cauldron have made it possible to recreate the assault lines of the Celtic soldiers.

The social system emphasised a "strict social hierarchy of which only the top social strata are visible to us. The 'princes'... resided in high citadels constituting the capital and the political heart of territories with a radius of about 40 kilometres (25 miles). But the geographical and topographical situation of these fortresses and the many imported objects which they received showed that they were also intended to control the important land and river routes used by convoys travelling to supply the Etruscan and especially the Greek markets." (Patrick Galliou, le Monde celtique).

During this same Hallstatt period, commercial relations intensified between the Celts and the peoples of the Mediterranean. This is evident from the magnificent treasure of the Celtic princess discovered in 1953 near Vix (Côte-d'Or), which contained several Greek- Etruscan objects and utensils. This Hallstatt culture was characterised by grandiose tombs, imposing fortresses (oppida) or lakeside towns such as the one at Biskupin in the central west of Poland. Excavations uncovered the tomb of a Celtic prince near Villingen, in the Black Forest (Magdelenberg mound). A sizeable funeral chamber comprising several elements of well conserved wood made it possible to date the tomb and the burial mound to 577 BC. In one of the several tombs making up the Magdelenberg mound, an Iberian belt buckle was found, demonstrating once again the relationship that existed between the centre and the rest of Europe.

Consequently, the oppidum, always located on an important commercial route, assumed considerable importance. Examples of oppida include de Manching in Bavaria or Bibracte on Mont Beuvray in Saône-et- Loire. Both a centre for craftsmen and a seat of royal power, it certainly inspired envy.

The La Tène culture

The high-point of the Iron Age bears the name of the culture known as La Tène (taken from the name of a Swiss archaeological site near Lake Neuchâtel) marking the peak of the Celtic civilisation. Celtic art evolved, adopting many eastern motifs in the torcs, fibula, belt buckles, bracelets etc. The technique of the craftsmen seems remarkable; not only did they work with bronze and gold but also with glass and enamel.

In the 3rd and 4th centuries BC, Celtic tribes invaded the Greek-Roman world, taking possession of northern Italy, pillaging Rome (385) and penetrating Macedonia and Thessaly. Even Delphi was threatened in 279. Some reached Asia Minor (the Galatians). Others entered Spain or acquired Armorica.

England was occupied by the Britons with raids taking place in the Bronze Age. These migrations formed the origin of the term "Britannic Isles", used by

the Greek geographer Pytheas as early as the 4th century to designate what today is known as Great Britain.

This domination, however, was not to continue: The Celts soon disappeared into the countries that they had invaded and were assimilated into the populations of the lands they had conquered, notably in Spain and in the lands between the Rhine and the Danube, where the Germanic tribes got the upper hand. On the plains of the Po river, they submitted to Roman authority.

Only two territories succeeded in maintaining both their independence and their Celtic culture. These were Ireland and Gaul, although the latter was threatened by the growing power of the Romans who occupied the Mediterranean coast from 120 BC. It should be noted, however, that in England, Wales and especially Scotland, Romanization was relatively superficial, allowing the old Celtic culture to be preserved.

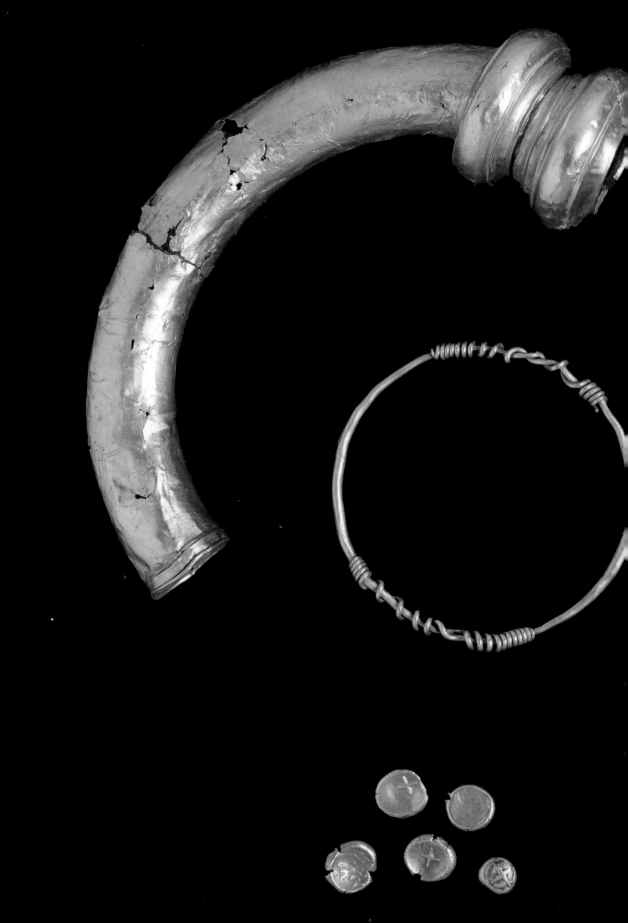

It is Greek and Latin authors who have revealed to us the existence of the Celtic world. The Greeks used the term *Keltoïs* to describe the Celts and the Romans used Celtae. In *The Conquest of Gaul*, Julius Caesar himself describes the Gallic religion in some detail. It was not until the 7th century AD that the great pagan myths of the Celts were written down for the first time, by monks. In fact, the Celts were always somewhat reserved with regard to writing. The druids, guardians of the religious traditions, likewise forbade putting in writing anything that dealt with religion. It is they who maintained a particularly lively oral tradition.

The discovery of a number of utensils and religious objects, such as weapons, helmets, jewellery etc., has given us a more profound knowledge of Celtic mythology. The cauldron of Gundestrup, for example, dating from the 1st century BC, represents Cernunnos, the horned god, reigning on the sacred faun, and Teutates, the god of the tribe. There are also many representations in stone of Sucellos, god of death and of hell. Precious evidence has also been obtained from tombs, bronze and stone statues and from coins (appearing as early as the 2nd century BC).

The Gallic Gods

Our knowledge of the Gallic religion has, to a great extent, been romanized. The druids themselves, long since popularised in elementary schools, have maintained their air of mystery in this regard. "It is in the oak woods that the druids have their sanctuaries..." reported Pliny the Elder in his *Natural History*. Apart from the long white robe and the golden billhook used for gathering the sacred mistletoe ("which cured everything" according to Pliny), we have no detailed knowledge of them.

Protectors of the traditions, educators of the young and guardians of the sacred word, the druids presided over religious life and dispensed justice. They were also soothsayers and magicians. And they performed human and animal sacrifices. This undoubtedly helped to reinforce their authority, making them at least equal to the King of the Celts, over whom they seemed to wield the power of life and death.

We know that the Gallic religion involved human sacrifices but these remained rare in spite of what was written by the ancient authors:

"We also see those suffering from serious illnesses, those who risk their lives in combat or otherwise, sacrificing or wishing to sacrifice human victims and using the ministry of the druids for these sacrifices; in fact, they think that the only way to appease the immortal gods is to replace the life of one man with the life of another and it was sacrifices of this type that were a public institution. Some tribes had huge baskets made of twisted wicker into which they placed living men. They set the baskets on fire with the men falling victim to the flames" (Julius Caesar, *The Conquest of Gaul*).

Sacred woods, sanctuaries and nature cults

In his work *Le Monde antique*, Maurice Meuleau states: "It is thus thanks to the evidence passed onto us by the old cultures of the Celts of Ireland, Wales and Brittany in their legendary narratives and folklore, that we can appreciate that the sacred world of the Celts of Gaul was as foreign as possible to Roman ideas... The Celts certainly had their major gods with relatively imprecise personalities yet, to an even greater extent, they recognised innumerable sacred manifestations in natural phenomena. The cults of the fertility goddesses, the 'Mothers' and the cults of sacred animals, trees and springs undoubtedly formed the essential part of religious life. There were few temples. Instead there were open-air, sacred enclosures where the faithful gathered for ceremonies, such as the collecting of mistletoe and the performing of bloody animal and even human sacrifices..."

Animal bones, remains of wooden statues and broken weapons have been discovered at many Celtic sites such as those at Goloring or Hochdorf in Germany, Gournay in France or Hayling Island in Great Britain.

One of the main difficulties in identifying Gallic gods is that they are often poorly defined. Their aspect or symbolism sometimes change according to the region or tribe. The Gauls worshipped fifty warrior gods compared to the one Roman god, Mars, but the attributes of these deities varied according to local customs.

Taranis, god of the wheel

The symbolic attributes of Taranis, principle deity of the Gauls, were forging and the sun wheel. He can be compared to the Taranis depicted on the Gundestrup cauldron.

Following pages
Pectoral of wheels and birds

This bronze dates from the Hallstatt period, 6th century BC.

23

Even if the Gallic pantheon seems to have included several hundred gods, we know of only a few. Latin authors have not made the task any easier for us by rather too quickly assimilating Gallic gods to their Roman equivalents – a phenomenon quickly amplified by the conquest and the rapid blossoming of the Gallic-Roman civilisation.

Originally, the Gauls venerated nature and the elements. There were different cults corresponding to the forces of nature. The water cult – rivers, streams, springs, fountains – was undoubtedly one of the most frequently practised. The equestrian goddess Epona, who presided over the fertility of the soil, was the main divinity. Altars marked the places where an underground river gushed forth. Nemausus, the god of the sacred spring, was associated with the town of Nîmes. Lakes and marshes could also appear as magical places. Objects for worship, weapons, chariots and cauldrons, perhaps with offerings for the gods, have been discovered in Switzerland (Lake Neuchâtel) and in Wales (Lake Llyn Fawr).

Many Latin inscriptions attest to the existence of tree gods: Fagus (beech), Buxenus (box tree), Robur (hard oak). The god Vosegus symbolised the magic power of the forests of the Vosges. The cult of the trees and forests assumed considerable importance. Possibly associated with the universe of the night, it was all the more significant and inspired fear. The ancestral fears supported animist beliefs and favoured the birth of new divinities, sometimes formidable.

The Gauls were dedicated to a true animal cult. In *Hommes et dieux de la Gaule*, Henri-Paul Eydoux describes a Gallic cemetery at Mont Granet (Marne), where the tomb of a stag was found that had been buried just like a human. In addition to the stag, many other animals were also considered sacred: the bull, boar, bear, horse (here we are reminded of the horse with the human head, adorned with a type of crown, from the burial place of the princess of Reinheim), ram, raven, birds of prey, serpent with a ram's head, dog or wolf etc. Jean Chevalier and Alain Gheerbrant in their *Dictionnaire des symboles*, stress that dogs were associated with the world of warriors. They add, "To compare a hero to a dog was to do him an honour, to pay homage to his value as a warrior." A bull figures on the Gallic-Roman monument of Nautes, found under Notre Dame – the *Tarvos Trigaranus* associated with three cranes. Bulls with three horns also appear here and there. The bulls of Irish epics come to mind here, often symbolising the warrior. Arduina, who reigned over the Ardennes, was the goddess of wild boars. Depictions of boars also decorate shields, warriors' helmets and coins.

Under Roman influence, the anthropomorphic tendencies were accentuated and new gods joined the Gallic pantheon, rich in animal and natural figures.

In his work, Caesar mentioned Mercury as the first autochthonous god. Sometimes his appearance differed from that of his Greek-Roman model. He actually appeared with the features of a more mature man and not of a young athlete with winged feet but his powers remained the same. A civilising god, Mercury preserved and safeguarded. Some historians link him to Teutates, Esus and Lug. Rosmerta, the goddess of fertility, is associated with him.

Minerva, who is also mentioned by Julius Caesar, seems to correspond to Belisama, "the shining one", but a version of her is also reincarnated in the Irish Brigid. Apollo, Mars and Vulcan also have their Gallic equivalents.

Taranis, god of the sky and of lightning, had the wheel and lightning flash as his symbol. He was feared and often demanded human sacrifices. He was assimilated to the Roman god Jupiter and the Germanic god Thor. One plaque on the Gundestrup cauldron represents a figure holding the cosmic wheel.

Teutates was the god of the tribes and protected the warriors. Human sacrifices were made in his honour by plunging the head of the victim into a vat until the person died. This deity, of which Caesar spoke at length in *The Conquest of Gaul*, evokes Mars, symbol of war, but also Mercury, the protector of merchants and travellers. He is often compared to the Germanic god Wotan and could also show himself to be bloodthirsty towards enemy armies. He is sometimes associated with the practice of "severed heads", a theme often dealt with by Gallic sculptors. An example of this is the head of stone found in the oppidum at Entremont in Provence, or the skulls on pillars at the sanctuary of Roquepertuse.

Esus, god of the earth and the forests, appears as a quiet traveller in the countryside, occupied with cutting bushes or pruning trees. Perhaps he was preparing the ritual hangings, which he performed very particularly. It was the Latin poet Lucan who revealed this detail to us.

We must, however, guard against blindly following the ancient authors, as their view of the Celtic customs tends to be rather subjective and biased.

Esus was sometimes identified as Mercury, as was the god Lug. He is seen notably to appear on the Gallic-Roman monument of Nautes, exhumed in Paris.

Lug, god of trade, was similar to the Roman Mercury. He gave his name to the town of Lyon (Lugdunum), which was dedicated to him, as well as to other European towns such as Leiden in The Netherlands, Leipzig or Liegnitz (Legnica) in Silesia. He is represented as having the traits of a barbarian (like Esus), accompanied by a raven. He possesses the attributes of a hammer and a serpent with a ram's head. He is also found in a quite different form in Ireland, where he protects travellers.

Sucellos, god of the earth and of hell, often appears surrounded by serpents. He sometimes brandishes a hammer – called the "Good Striker" – ito help him despatch the dying, as in the theory of Jan de Vries. Associated with the goddess Nantosuelta, Sucellos also symbolised fertility and abundance. His hammer served as an agricultural tool for fertilising the earth. He was perhaps Dis Pater, father of all Gauls, of whom Julius Caesar spoke.

Cernunnos, the god of the stag wood, wore around his neck a torc (rigid collar) made of gold or bronze and in one of his hands held a snake with a ram's head. Half human, half animal, he was revered by the Gauls, who often portrayed him with his legs crossed, in the company of other deities. Cernunnos reigned over the world of animals.

This strange creature is found in many Celtic representations, notably on the Gundestrup cauldron (made in the north of Gaul or much further east on the borders of Galatia, we do not know exactly how it came to be there, but it was found in a pothole in Jutland) dating from the 1st century BC, or on a statuette found at Rheims (Gallic-Roman period) but also in Burgundy and in England.

Cernunnos evokes the mysterious Dis Pater who had a goddess mother for company ("All Gauls claim to be descended from Dis Pater: it is, so they say, a tradition of the druids. It is based on this belief that they measure time, not according to the number of days, but the number of nights... " Caesar, *The Conquest of Gaul*).

Sun god of fertility, Cernunnos has the torc, the purse and the sack of grain. Jean-Jacques Hatt states, "Each year, at the time when Cernunnos was supposed to turn back into Esus, the Gauls went to the forest to hunt stag and deer, which they sacrificed and skinned. They then clothed themselves in the fresh hides and abandoned themselves to frantic dance. Then they stripped themselves of the hides to celebrate the return of Esus to the earth" (*Essay on the evolution of the Gallic religion*). It is easy to see the symbolic significance of such practices: by sacrificing the deer and spilling its blood, the hunter warrior took on the virtues and life force of the animal.

These pagan rites were performed in several regions, in Lozère, Corrèze, Switzerland and Bavaria and later provoked strong reactions from the church authorities, who denounced such actions. This was undoubtedly because they evoked pagan relics but also because they contributed to reinforcing one of the most prolific myths of European folklore, imbued with Satanism: the infernal hunt, the name of which changed according to the region (Hennequin hunt in Normandy, hunt of the flying phantom in Brittany, hunt of King Arthur in les Landes, wild hunt in Alsace etc.)

In the stories of Gallic and Irish mythology, the hunt often permits the mortal or the divine hunter to penetrate into the kingdom of the hereafter.

Maponus, "the young man with gracious traits", is similar to Apollo and corresponds to the Irish god Aengus. Some specialists also link him with Borvo or Bormanus, the Gallic god of springs, and with Belenos, who symbolised sunlight.

Ogmios, god of eloquence, evokes Hercules but he does not seem to be endowed with the legendary strength of the Greek hero. A small figure with a bald head, he is clothed in an animal hide, proudly sporting a bludgeon. In Irish mythology, he becomes the god Ogma, inventor of messages in ogham. Some inscriptions using this alphabetical writing system have been found, made with cuts and strokes engraved on stone.

Smertrios seems very close to Ogmios. He is likewise equipped with a bludgeon. He succeeded in defeating the infernal dog that Taranis had sent against the goddess mother but he did not manage to repel a further assault and was transformed, with Esus and the goddess, into cranes. It is these which adorn the Tarvos Trigaranus of the monument of the Nautes. Having sacrificed three bulls, they regained their human form.

Three cranes, three bulls... this reveals a trend in Celtic mythology, both on the islands and the continent: the taste for three-headed deities (figures with three heads, goddess mothers in threes etc.). The three-headed busts on the Gallic-Roman vase at Bavay are a good example of this.

Myths and Gods of Ireland

Although well-integrated into the Roman Empire, the Gallic Celts continued to worship their gods, even if Roman beliefs progressively amalgamated with theirs. It was mainly the appearance of Christianity and its adoption by the Romans which brought about the progressive decline of the ancient religions. Even in Ireland, which was never really under Roman control, the influence of Christianity soon made itself felt. Paradoxically, this symbiosis between paganism and Christianity, manifested later in the legends of King Arthur, made it possible in Ireland and Wales to safeguard a large number of Celtic legends. From the 6th century onwards, the monks were able to rewrite the stories of mythology without anyone suspecting them of paganism, because care was taken to distinguish druids and witches from the poets who travelled the country singing about the exploits of the legendary heroes. Besides this, druids resisted much longer in Ireland, Wales and Cornwall than on the continent and did not disappear until around 500 AD. This oral tradition of the bards has allowed the myths to be carried down to us. Inscriptions and votive tablets, Medieval manuscripts and popular legends also constitute very important sources for the study of Celtic mythology on the islands.

We do not know when the Celts were established in Great Britain but it seems that the Gaels settled there as early as the 8th century BC. Five centuries later, they were joined by the Britons, who progressively drove them out. A little later, other Celtic tribes, notably the Belgians, took their turn to cross the channel, pushing the Gaels back further and forcing them to cross to Ireland. Paradoxically, although Ireland was the only country to remain Celtic until the Middle Ages, it is also the region where the origins of the population remain the most imprecise. Gaelic and Irish mythology is the richest and most characteristic but British mythology, including that from Kymry in Wales, must not be ignored. Even though the deities are often the same, the names change. The goddess Dana, mother of the Celtic pantheon, becomes Dôn in Wales. Dagda, the brother of Dana, becomes Math in Wales. Bile, the god of hell in Ireland, is called Beli; Goibniu becomes Govannon.

Dana (or Danu), mother of the gods, brings fertility to the land. Her husband was Bile, the legendary ancestor of the Irish. The brother of Dana is called Dagda, "the good god", who is also revealed as a powerful warlord. It is he who leads into battle the tribes of the goddess Dana (Tuatha Dé Danann), a race of heroes descended from Dana and Bile.

Dagda, the most important god in Irish mythology, was armed with an iron bludgeon with which he could kill several men with a single blow but he could also bring the dead back to life simply by touching them with the other end of his bludgeon. Master of the elements, he set himself up as head of the tribes and extended his authority to the druids. Lover of Morrigan, the goddess of war, Dagda, associated with abundance, had a formidable appetite. In the fight against the Fomorian sea demons, Dagda entered their camp one day and was met by quite an extraordinary test. The Fomorian had prepared a mixture for him made of milk, flour and fat, a sort of porridge. To this potion, they added a large number of cows, sheep and goats, in sufficient quantity to feed almost a hundred starving men. The Fomorian gave Dagda the choice: either he must eat all of it down to the last bite or he would meet a terrible end. Dagda did not need to be told twice and swallowed the entire contents of the cauldron in one gulp. This was not the extent of his talents, however, because this singular warrior possessed a magic cauldron and played an enchanted harp that could cause death or sleep. An ambivalent deity who brought life and death, Dagda ("the good") could also be evil.

Midir or Mider was one of the sons of Dagda. He was represented as having the traits of a beautiful young man. Often associated with the other world, he was also the husband of the beautiful Etain.

Cernunnos of the three faces

Cernunnos, the "horned one", reigned over the animal world and the forests. God of fertility, he was often at the head of the wild hunt. He can be seen notably on one of the plaques of the Gundestrup cauldron. Sitting cross-legged, Cernunnos wears a torc with rams'heads and holds two serpents in his hands.

Lug (Lleu in Wales) is similar to the Gallic Lug. Sun god par excellence, he proved himself as one of the supreme entities and one of the fiercest warriors in Ireland. Lug fought against the Fomorian, who were commanded by his grandfather Balor, during the second battle of Mag Tured and defended the kingdom of Ulster against invaders. God of trades, Lug is sometimes named Samildanach ("multiple craftsman" or "one who knows many things"). This is hardly surprising, seen that he represents the blacksmith, carpenter, metalworker, doctor, artist and combatant. Thanks to his incomparable talents, Lug was able to penetrate the royal city of Tara just before the first battle of Mag Tured. In fact, he replied to the soldier who denied him access – on the grounds that the arts and techniques possessed by Lug were already represented in Tara – that he was the only one capable of employing these techniques in one single day and in an unbeatable fashion!

Nuada (Nudd in Welsh mythology), husband of the war goddess Morrigan, participated in the first battle of Mag Tured, where he lost a hand. Diancecht, the god of medicine, offered him a new one made of silver. Nuada was not satisfied with this, however, and asked Miach, son of Diancecht, to make him a hand of flesh and blood. This he did but the god of medicine, jealous of his son's talents, ended up killing Miach. Nuada perished in the second battle of Mag Tured, surprised by the exterminating eye of Balor.

Ogma, symbol of power and eloquence, invented the ogham script. An amber chain related the Ogma language to those who listened. Son of Dagda, he was also a brave warrior who accompanied the dead warriors to Síd, their new dwelling place. This was the invisible kingdom of the spirits, fairies and monsters, Annwyn (or Annfwn, the abyss in Welsh) or Avalon of the legends of King Arthur. It must be noted, as pointed out by Jean Markale, that the Other World of the Celts is not the sinister, pallid place known, for example, by the Greeks or the Romans. Celtic warriors considered the world of the dead as a sort of extension of their life on earth. Did they not rest there for a while waiting for their reincarnation? In Celtic legends there are constant allusions to combatants, dead on the field of battle, brought back to life the day after. Sometimes, however, the other world revealed a worrying universe populated by hideous creatures in the image of Bodb, the crow goddess of desolation: white dogs with red ears, skeletons mounted on red-brown horses or blood-covered sorceresses.

Balor was the chief of the Fomorian, the ancient sea gods who oppressed Ireland before being crushed by the Tuatha Dé Danann. Endowed with just one eye, he possessed remarkable powers but, nevertheless, perished at the battle of Mag Tured at the hand of his own grandson. This fate had been predicted to him and he took the precaution of locking away his only daughter Ethlinn in a tower of crystal. This act was nevertheless in vain, as a druidess introduced Cian to the beautiful Ethlinn and the inevitable happened. When Balor learned that his daughter had given birth to triplets, he ordered them to be destroyed but one of the infants escaped this curse. Taken in by Goibniu, the blacksmith god, the small child grew and soon became the god Lug. He killed his grandfather with his magic sling. Lug chose the right moment and slung his stone so accurately that it hit the eye of Balor, assuring the victory of the Tuatha Dé Danann over the Fomorian.

Goibniu (Govannon in Wales), the blacksmith god, made the most fearsome weapons thanks to his dexterity and his enchanted hammer. He also made beer and barley beer for celebrations.

Bron (Bendigeidfran or Bran in Wales), son of Lir, the sea god, and of his wife Iwerydd, possessed a magic cauldron which brought the dead back to life, without giving them back the power of speech. He must not be confused with Bran the navigator. In the Welsh version, the giant Bran quarrelled with Matholwch, the king of Ireland, who had married his sister Branwen and humiliated her. Having raised an army, Bran left for Ireland. The shock was terrible and all the Irish perished in the battle. Bran, mortally wounded, asked for his head to be severed. According to legend, his head was taken to London where it was buried facing towards Europe to protect Great Britain from her enemies. King Arthur made use of the relic to accomplish his exploits.

Manannan mac Lir (Manawydan in Welsh mythology), brother of Bron, definitely takes his name from the Isle of Man. God of the sea and navigation, he was also a formidable magician. His wife, Fand, one of great beauty, fell in love with the hero Cuchulainn. Manannan made use of his cape to separate them and prevented them meeting again. He was also able to calm the waves and unleash storms. Manannan had three legs which can be seen on the coat of arms of the Isle of Man.

The unknown god

Demonstrating an amazing hieratic aspect, this statuette bears witness to the artistic sense of the Celts. Sitting cross-legged with the torc around his neck, this figure doubtless represents a legendary god or hero. The surviving eye is made of enamel.

Aengus or Oengus, son of Dagda and Boann, the water deity, was the god of love. An incomparable beauty, Aengus sought the company of birds, which he transformed into passionate kisses.

Brigid (sometimes called Brigit), daughter of Dagda, represented poetry, medicine and trades. She blessed women with fertility. Brigid and her two sisters are sometimes considered as one deity. She can be compared to Minerva. In Brittany, she was called Brigantia and ruled over the Brigantes. In Irish mythology, Brigid was the wife of Bres, who was a formidable tyrant. She was so popular that she survived under the guise of a Christian saint: Saint Brigid of Kildare.

There were other goddesses who were by no means as nice: Morrigan, the queen of the phantoms, who appeared as a raven on the fields of battle; Badb, the crow; Macha, another deity of war; or even Nemain, whose name evoked misfortune. Just before losing his life in a final battle, the hero of Ulster, Cuchulainn, perceived a washer woman, in tears, washing blood-covered clothing. It was indeed a bad omen, because it was, in fact, Nemain. In Armorica, they have long kept the memory of this episode by recalling the "washer woman of the night", phantoms condemned to work for eternity. Deadly creatures, bringers of bad news, these washer women attracted poor wretches and inflicted terrible torments upon them.

The Great Cycles of Irish Legend

All the manuscripts which have come down to us relating to the great stories of the hero epics of Irish literature are from the Middle Ages. Some were written in the 7th century but they have been lost or destroyed. Others date from a later period. *The Leabhar Gabhâla (The Book of Invasions)* describes, with the use of many images, the legendary origins of Ireland, mixing pieces of genuine history, Celtic myths and Christian additions. Most of the texts have been revised, enriched and sometimes modified over the course of the centuries. Their primordial interest lies in the fact that they contain elements incontestably older than the period when they were written.

Successive invasions

The jewel of Irish mythology, *The Book of Invasions*, relates the story of successive invasions of Ireland occurring since the Flood. Based on monastery writings of the 6th and 7th centuries AD, *The Book of Invasions* reappeared in the 12th century.

Cessair, the magician queen, was the first to grace the soil of the great Erin. Descended directly from Noah, she perished with all her family, despite her fabulous powers.

Coming from Greece around 2600 BC, Partholon disembarked in Ireland with a small escort. He and his companions did an enormous amount of work, improving the soil, raising cattle and even creating three lakes. They prospered for a time – five thousand years according to the legend – but were finally annihilated, not by their enemies, the Fomorian race of sea giants that populated the Irish coast (sometimes described as beings with goat heads), but by a terrible epidemic.

Several hundred years later new invaders came, the Nemed, but it was not long before they were almost all massacred by the Fomorian.

Around 2400 BC, the Fir Bolg appeared. They came from Greece and, as it would seem, accomplished a considerable task. They instituted a monarchy and split the country into five provinces: Ulster, Connaught, Munster, Leinster and Meath. The Fir Bolg, however, bowed down to a new race of invaders arriving from the north: the Tuatha Dé Danann. They, the divine race, had a trump card and more than one trick up their sleeve: the magic cauldron of Dagda which never ran dry and could also bring the dead back to life; the invincible Sword of Nuada that recounted the feats of arms of its possessor when removed from its scabbard; the spear of Lug; and the stone of Fâl (or Fail) which screamed when a King of Ireland sat upon it. Georges Dumézil in *Mythe et épopée* relates the three talismans – cauldron, sword-spear and magic stone – to the sacred objects of the scythe tradition (goblet, axe and plough). A link could also be established with the story of the Grail (goblet, spear, sword and tool).

The stone of Fâl, sometimes called Cromm Cruaich ("the curve of the mound") was destroyed by Saint Patrick, who buried it in the ground with the aid of his cross.

Legend has it that the Fir Bolg reached the islands of Aran, to the west of Ireland, and that they prospered there. Today, we can still see the remains of the Dun Aengus fort at Irishmore.

The battles of Mag Tured

The Tuatha Dé Danann were perhaps the constructors of the megaliths. They lived in Ireland during the second millennium BC before the Gaels appeared. The triumph of the tribes of the Goddess Dana did not happen overnight and it took two bloody battles to assure their supremacy.

The initial confrontation with the Fir Bolg took place at Mag Tured (Moyra). During the battle, the Tuatha Dé Danann gained the advantage but their King, Nuada, lost his right hand. He had to give up the place to Bres, the son of Elatha, King of the Fomorian, whose kingdom was situated beyond the seas. Bres behaved like a tyrant, overwhelming the Tuatha and favouring the Fomorian in a shameless fashion. When Nuada retook the throne, Miach having made him a new hand, Bres took refuge with the Fomorian. Conflict became inevitable. The second battle of Mag Tured was terrible. Lug, Commander-in-Chief of Dana's troops, assembled the gods and distributed the roles: Dagda used his bludgeon, Goibniu forged blades and spears, Ogma breathed in the energy necessary for the victory and Diancecht cared for the wounded.

Although the preparations for combat took seven years, the battles themselves did not drag on forever. When Ogma and Nuada perished, Lug decided to throw himself into the thick of things and confront his grandfather, the giant Cyclops Balor, easily the most formidable of the Fomorian – using his eye, he could devastate his enemies just by gazing upon them. When the battle was at its fiercest, Lug approached Balor and, with his magic sling, managed to shoot a stone into his eye. It went so deep that Balor's eye passed through his skull and felled the Fomorian who were behind him, deciding the outcome of the battle. At the same time, Lug chanted incantations at the Fomorian; using only one eye, one arm and one leg, he managed to force the enemy to flee.

The victory of the Tuatha Dé Danann was total. The Fomorian were pushed back to the sea and everywhere Morrigan proclaimed the success of the tribes of the goddess Dana. The triumph was completed when Lug and Dagda, joined by Ogma who had been brought back to life, found the sacred harp, which had been stolen by the Fomorian. Bres was taken prisoner but escaped death by providing the Tuatha with the secrets of agriculture. From this point on, the cows of Ireland would always have milk and the harvests would be eternally plentiful. Shortly afterwards, however, the Tuatha had to surrender their place to the Milesians, the sons of Milé, who came from Spain and celebrated their victory at Tara, the royal capital.

Celtic deity

This is undoubtedly one of the many goddess mothers found all over in Gaul, symbolising fertility and protecting the home. Often made of stone or terracotta, they highlighted the importance that the Gauls attached to motherhood. This particular example is wearing a horn of plenty. The person sat cross-legged at her side is possibly Cernunnos.

The great poet Amergin decided that the gentle Eriu (or Erin) who welcomed the Milesians should give her name to the country. He also ordained that the Tuatha Dé Danann disappear underground to join the realms of the fairies. They live under the hills where mortals can go and pay homage. It is this which perhaps explains the location of sanctuaries on the hillocks and plains of Ireland. The sons of Milé, ancestors of the Gaels, remained masters of Irish soil.

The legend of Midir and Etain

Among the mythological narratives, the romance between Midir, son of Dagda, and Etain is particularly interesting. Midir, unlike his father Dagda, seduced by virtue of his beauty and sought the company of women. Having abandoned his first wife, Fuammach, Midir directed his attention towards Etain. Alas, Fuammach, who was very jealous, decided to attack her rival, grazing her with the branch of a red sorb tree and changing her into a pond.

The beautiful Etain was also subjected to further misfortunes as the pond dried out and gave birth to a sort of larva which then became a superb, purple-coloured insect. The fluttering of its wings seemed so soft, and the sparkling of its eyes so brilliant that Midir was able to recognise her despite the metamorphosis. Fuammach did not admit defeat and unleashed a windstorm that swept Etain far away to a place outside Ireland.

Seven years later, Aengus, the adopted son of Midir, took in the insect and gave her shelter. Once again, Fuammach demonstrated her perfidy and brought misfortune to Etain. Etain was, in fact, swallowed by the wife of an Ulster warrior and was reincarnated much later with the traits of the wife of a King of Ireland. Aengus set off in search of Fuammach, found her after several years and cut her throat, thus avenging the unhappy love of Midir and Etain.

Cuchulainn, the hero of Ulster

Another grand heroic cycle retraces the great deeds of the heroes of Ulster at the time of Conchobar, King of Ireland, who, according to tradition, reigned at the beginning of our era. In fact, the characteristic details contained in medieval texts actually evoke an earlier period, namely the period of La Tène, the 3rd to 2nd century BC. The texts, one of the most famous of which is called Cooley's Cattle Raid, are from the 7th and 8th centuries and were rewritten by monks in the 12th century.

Cuchulainn was the son of Dechtiré, daughter of the druid Cathbad and sister of the king Conchobar. His father was apparently Fergus Mac Roich but his real father was none other than Lug, who had loved Dechtiré in the Other World. At birth, he was named Sêtanta and he received a select education supervised by the warrior princess Scathach, who taught him many secrets.

At the age of seven, he killed the ferocious guard dog of Culann, blacksmith of Ulster, with his bare hands. To compensate for his loss, Sêtanta made an offer to Culann to replace his dog until he could tame another one. This is how he got his last name of Cú Chulainn ("the dog of Culann"). Following this initial exploit, he attacked three warrior magicians and massacred all their supporters. His legendary strength and his intelligence enabled him to accomplish many great feats but his warrior spirit could also sometimes be a disadvantage. When he became angry, he trembled violently, drops of blood issued from his hair and his face became deformed.

The Gundestrup cauldron

Made of moulded silver plates, the cauldron or vase of Gundestrup was probably produced in a workshop in Gaul or even further east, in Hungary or on the borders of Galatia, in the 1st century BC. Found in a pothole in Jutland, Denmark, this receptacle was used for ritual celebrations. With the many representations of deities on its panels, it serves as a good illustration of the major themes of Celtic mythology. On the inside, a human sacrifice is portrayed.

Cuchulainn was, however, very forward with women, who happily returned his affections. The husband of Emer, he also became the lover of the beautiful Fand, wife of Manannan mac Lir; of Uatach, the daughter of Scathach; and of the femme fatale Aoife, skilled combatant who was none other than the sister of Scathach. From their love was born Conlai, a boy whom Cuchulainn killed one day in a hand-to-hand battle. It was only when he noticed the gold ring that the dead boy wore on his finger that Cuchulainn realised his tragic mistake.

Upon returning from an expedition, Cuchulainn, at the mercy of his warrior fury, even frightened King Conchobar. In order to placate him, the king sent a cortege of fifty naked young women to meet him. Quite thrown by the spectacle, the hero was spellbound. Advantage was taken of this state to plunge him into three tanks of cold water: the first burst, the second started to boil but, in the third, the water finally turned tepid. The strategy had worked.

The most spectacular feat of arms of the hero Cuchulainn was undoubtedly the campaign that he undertook to defend the kingdom of Ulster, which was threatened by a powerful coalition commanded by Queen Medb. The magic bull of Cooley, coveted by rival clans, served as the pretext to start this long war. Ulster thus found herself in direct conflict with the coalition armies of the four other kingdoms of Ireland (Connaught, Munster, Leinster and Meath).

Medb was careful to start her offensive at a time when the people of Ulster were not able to defend themselves, paralysed by a curse of the goddess Macha.

With only his courage to guide him, Cuchulainn fought the invaders almost single-handed. Thanks to encouragement from Lug and his natural ability, he at first managed to contain the army of Queen Medb but, in the end, she proved to be stronger. Her allies, the three Calatin witches, used their spells to inflict several decisive blows against Cuchulainn, who, nevertheless, continued fighting until his strength failed him. Wounded in the stomach, he attached himself to a menhir so as not to fall down in front of his enemies and died standing with his weapon in his hand. Morrigan, taking the appearance of a crow, immediately came and perched on his shoulder.

Celtic chariot

This chariot was found in the funeral hoard of the tomb of the princess of Hochdorf.

This period of Cuchulainn, of which we are describing only a very small part here, inspired many mythical stories and influenced the legend of King Arthur. The person himself, hero without compare, has kept an important place in the tradition of Irish legend.

Fíngen and Conn of the Hundred Battles

On the night of Samhain, it was possible to communicate with the hereafter and to reaffirm the connections between the living and the dead. Christianity adopted the same idea in celebrating All Saints. Samhain also marked the beginning of winter and of the New Year. Beltaine, the other Celtic celebration, on 1 May, marks the birth of summer and the opening of the pastures.

The etymology of the word can be traced back to Belenos and Bel, both symbolising light. On the night of Samhain, a fairy coming from the Síd (the other world of Irish legends) took a shine to Fíngen, druid and doctor of King Conchobar, and announced to him the imminent coming of a marvellous sovereign who would soon reign over Ireland: Conn of the Hundred Battles.

Fíngen was, without doubt, very upset, seeing as he was destined for higher functions, but he did not let it show. A long time rebel against the authority of the great king, in the end Fíngen submitted and rejoined the court. As for Conn of the Hundred Battles, he fell in love with an evil fairy, who made him forget his duties. Ireland suffered and Conn's son Art was obliged to come to the rescue. The young man had to undertake a perilous ocean voyage searching for Delbchaen, a beautiful young woman whom he married. The spell on Conn was then lifted at once and Ireland regained her prosperity.

Conle, another son of Conn, met with a tragic end. Seduced by an invisible woman, he stopped taking food and took off in search of his love. Conle boarded a crystal boat destined for a mysterious isle from which he never returned.

The fabulous voyages

Heroic quests, voyages to a perilous or frightening Other World are also favourite themes in Celtic mythology and the mythology of the whole world. We can generally conclude that these stories have a lot of points in common, probably because across images and traditions, they symbolise an absolute quest and tend to piece together the long development of the human soul. Very ancient myths retranscribed by the monks between the 5th and 8th centuries, these legends were enriched with Christian references in the image of Brendan, the Irish navigator saint.

Bran remains, without doubt, the most famous of the Irish navigators. It was a fairy who suggested that he take to the sea to discover the wonders of a world reputed to be inaccessible. Bran and his companions at once undertook a long voyage beyond the seas, valiantly supported by Manannan mac Lir, god of the tides. Upon reaching the Isle of Gaiety, they became disconcerted by the attitude of the inhabitants, who thought of nothing but laughing all day long. The following day, Bran reached the Isle of Women, where a blissful time awaited him. In order to moor the boat, all the navigators had to do was to seize a magic thread thrown to them by the queen of the island. Once on the island, Bran and his companions experienced a happiness marked with abundance and delight. They planned to stay on the island for just a year but, in reality, decades passed. When they started to feel homesick, they decided to return and succeeded in convincing the queen to allow them to leave. But she warned them not to set foot on land when they returned to Ireland. Forgetting this warning, after a long return voyage, one of the sailors stepped onto the shore and was immediately turned to ash. Bran wisely contented himself with hailing the fishermen on the shore and narrating his adventures. No-one recalled him except for an old man who remembered, in times past, having heard a story recounting his epic adventures. Bran decided to get under way and no-one ever saw him again.

Another voyage, which is somewhat reminiscent of the twelve labours of Hercules, had Brian and his two brothers as the protagonists. They had assassinated Cian. To atone for this crime, Lug demanded that they accomplish an almost impossible mission which consisted of bringing magic objects to Ireland: the apples from the silver garden, a roasting spit guarded by sea nymphs, the poisoned spear of the King of Persia, the golden pigs of King Asal, the horses and chariot of the King of Sicily, a healing pig skin from the Greek King etc. At the end of an exciting voyage, Brian succeeded in collecting all of these marvellous objects.

Head of a rod
This enigmatic face made of bronze dates from the period of La Tène II, 2nd century BC.

Now all that remained for him to do was overcome the obstacle of the last task: shouting out three times from the Mochean hill. The three brothers could not reach the summit of the hill and were injured in the attempt. Their father, Tuireann, implored Lug to lend him the pig skin to heal his sons. The god refused and the three brothers died in terrible suffering.

The strange legend of Maelduin tells of how this voyager, to avenge his assassinated father, undertook a fantastic voyage across the seas, discovering islands, some more extraordinary than others. Assisted by a druid, who used his science to help construct the vessel, Maelduin took to the open sea, accompanied by twenty men. Thus began an impressive odyssey, taking the crew from one surprise to the next. They came upon an island inhabited by giant, carnivorous ants that devoured a large part of the crew. On another island, Maelduin was confronted by horses with steel hooves. The Isle of Salmon, on the other hand, afforded them more hospitality and gave the navigators a chance to rest. Evil spells abounded on other islands: volcano eruptions, crying birds, giant pigs, living dead, jumping crabs, a sea of clouds, a mirage island etc. Then, on the high sea, Maelduin and his colleagues noticed a column of silver from which was hanging an immense net. To the great surprise of the crew, the vessel was able to clear a passage through the mesh of the net and one of the sailors even cut a piece from it. After a relatively peaceful passage to the country of women, Maelduin found his father's assassins and pardoned them. He then returned to Ireland and recounted his extraordinary story.

The Fenian myths

The Leinster cycle seemed very different to the myths cited above. The period involved seems to precede the appearance of Christianity in Ireland and relates to the 3rd and 4th centuries. These texts are no longer concerned with heroes or tribal deities but warlords, the fiana ("bands" or even "blonds") or fenians, who hired out their services to sovereigns. In both of the Gaelic countries, Ireland and Scotland, these stories were no longer the prerogative of the tribes but appeared on a country-wide level. These stories also grew considerably after the Saxon invasion in the 6th century. The writings were retranscribed in the 7th century.

The fiana take their name from Finn MacCool (sometimes called Finn Mac Cumail), their leader. He was the son of Cumhal ("the sky"). A hunter, poet and warrior all in one, Finn also possessed the talents of a diviner. He acquired this gift thanks to the druid Finegas who raised him. One day, he asked Finn to cook the Salmon of Knowledge, fished from the river Boyne. Finn did this but burned himself whilst preparing the fire. Bringing his finger to his mouth, he sucked the burn which had lightly brushed against the sacred fish. So Finegas allowed his young disciple to eat the salmon. Finn obtained wisdom and the "knowledge which illuminates". All he had to do was suck his thumb and the things he did not know would be revealed to him.

Finn confronted Goll, his rival, who had only one eye. He had, however, helped Finn to kill the witch Irnan. Finn also pursued Diarmaid, the son of Aengus the god of love. Diarmaid had actually taken off with the beautiful Grainne, Finn's betrothed. Grainne was the daughter of the powerful King of Ireland, Cormac Mac Airt. The lovers lived happily for a long time but had to escape many a trap set for them by the fiana who were pursuing them. After ten years, Diarmaid died, disembowelled by a bewitched boar. Finn could have saved him with his healing powers but he still wanted his revenge on account of Grainne and finally let him die. As for the young woman, she swore that she would take her revenge but Finn managed to seduce her.

Riding a grey horse, a gift from Abarta, Finn fought constantly at the head of his companions, although he did sometimes manage to rest in his palace or enjoy himself. One day, during a hunt with his dogs, he followed a magnificent stag which took him far away into the forest. The exhausted animal lay down on the ground to await its death. Instead of rushing at their prey, the dogs circled the animal and started yapping. Finn decided to spare the stag, which then assumed a human form, that of a very beautiful young woman. It was Sadb, whom a magician had bewitched. Finn decided to make her his mistress and the evil left her. Alas, Sadb disappeared one day, taken off by an evil genie. Despite all his efforts and even though he searched Ireland high and low many times, Finn was not able to find her. She had, however, given him a son Ossian ("little fawn"), who was to become one of the greatest Irish poets.

Ossian's exploits are proved worthy of those of his father. Whilst hunting, the young Ossian met Niamh, the daughter of the sea god Manannan mac Lir.

The Tarvos Trigaranus "Ox with three cranes"

Remains of a monument dedicated to Jupiter associating Gallic and Roman gods. The pillar of Nantes well illustrates the high regard in which the ox was held; it was a sacred animal of the Gallic-Romans. The animal also had the same status with the Irish, who considered it blessed by the gods. In Cooley's Cattle Raid, one of the episodes from the epic of the Ulster cycle, the magic ox of Cuailnge plays a predominant role.

Stonehenge

This collection of megaliths was built in the south of England, between Wales and Cornwall, on Salisbury Plain (Wiltshire). Older than the first Celtic civilisations, Stonehenge was probably constructed in several stages between 1800 and 1400 BC. The site was certainly used by the Celts for religious purposes, as were many menhirs, dolmens and raised stones in Ireland, Scotland and

She proposed to take him to the kingdom of her father, one of the Celtic paradises. This was an idyllic stay, even though Ossian had to confront various monsters.

After several decades, however, he started to feel homesick for Ireland. Thus Niamh entrusted him with her horse with the golden mane and silver hooves but warned him not to set foot upon the ground. Upon returning to his native soil, Ossian no longer recognised his country, which had changed a great deal. It had been cruelly battered.

The population seemed weak and miserable, bearing no resemblance to the heroic people he had once known. Meeting a group of poor wretches, who were having problems moving a pile of rocks, Ossian offered to help them and pushed the stones without a problem, aided by his trusty horse. Alas, his saddle slipped and he fell to the ground. When he got up, he realised that he had become a fragile old man, nearly blind. The magic had ceased to work.

In a Christian addition to the legend, Ossian meets Saint Patrick, who explains to him how Ireland

changed during his absence. So the bard decides to take his lyre and sing the exploits of the gods and heroes of bygone times. The myth of Ossian has been perpetuated, particularly thanks to the Scottish poet James McPherson who, at the end of the 18th century, rediscovered Gaelic stories from ancient times thanks to the Poems of Ossian. These texts, of which McPherson was actually the author, excited the imagination of the Romantics and aroused the enthusiasm of many writers including Goethe, Herder, Germaine de Staël, Chateaubriand and Lord Byron.

Another protagonist of the cycle was Conan, the brother of Goll. If one is to believe the collection of stories from the 12th century, The Colloquy of the Ancients, which portrays him as a quick-tempered warrior, his influence appears more negative. There is no doubt that the American Romantic Robert Howard had him in mind when he created Conan the Barbarian in the thirties. This Cimmerian, living at the dawn of history, heralded the future success of fantasy literature. An illustrated volume and several films from the nineteen-eighties each depict the memory of Conan in their own way.

Armorica etc. It is probable that the alignments of the menhirs were linked to sun cults, while the dolmens and the covered alleys constituted vast tombs. Several hypotheses have been offered on the purpose of Stonehenge: cemetery, place of sacrifice, astronomical observatory. Although there is no doubt that this was a sacred place, there is uncertainty amongst the experts as to its exact purpose.

Legends of Wales

Welsh literature relating the myths of the gods and heroes is noticeably more recent than the Irish stories: the most ancient texts date from the 10th century. They are inspired more by the Christian religion which characterises them. Most of the deities are, however, the same and many of the legends are similar. The main body of text, composed between the 11th and 14th centuries, is entitled The Four Branches of the Mabinogion and transcribes more ancient mythical traditions.

The dominant god is called Gwydion, son of Don. He is the chief of the children of Don, a divine tribe reminiscent of the Irish Tuatha Dé Danann. The children of Don are opposed to the children of Llyr, the divine competing dynasty. Their rivalry occupies an important place in Welsh mythology. Civilising god par excellence, Gwydion protects the arts and also reveals himself as an exceptional warlord. Like the Irish Ogma, he is also an excellent orator. He has a sister Arianrhod ("silver wheel") with whom he carries on incestuous relations. The main actors in these stories and legends are the gods, heroes and marvellous animals. There are many supernatural and fantastic elements which confer on the stories undeniable literary qualities as well as a singularly captivating symbolic power.

Pwyll and Rhiannon

The First Branch of the Mabinogion retraces the adventures of the Pwyll family, in which Rhiannon and Pryderi play a particularly important part. Pwyll, Prince of Dyfed, allied himself to the tribes of the god Llyr and visited the other world (Annwn). There he proved his great courage and imposed his law, attracting the good graces of Arawn, the master of the place. He also acquired his surname of Pen Annwn ("lord of the hereafter"). Their first meeting, however, did not bode well for the future. Whilst hunting a stag, Pwyll had encroached on the territory of the Arawn hunt and taken the hide of the animal. He was encircled by a pack of vicious white dogs with red eyes and had to accept the proposition made to him by Arawn: to change his appearance and become the ruler of the other world, while the master of the other world

replaced him at the head of the kingdom of Dyfed. Pwyll performed his task brilliantly and killed Hafgan, the enemy of Arawn. Upon returning home, he found that his kingdom had grown more beautiful, as if it had undergone a metamorphosis.

Pwyll then married Rhiannon, the goddess of horsemen, who rode her magic horse and could not be followed. They had a son called Pryderi. A dark drama occurred, however, and Rhiannon was accused of assassinating her own son. Condemned to remain at the doors of the palace and to transport anyone who wished to travel, Rhiannon thus became the patron of travellers. Even once her son returned, the spell continued. The very model of level-headedness, Rhiannon conserved her natural kindness and pardoned her enemies. She was always surrounded by marvellous birds, emissaries of the other world, which could put the living to sleep and waken the dead.

As for Pryderi, he succeeded his father at the head of the kingdom of Dyfed and reigned in the other world. Concerned about the happiness of his mother, whom he had involuntarily given great cause for worry, Pryderi encouraged her to remarry Manawydan, the son of the sea god Llyr.

Branwen, daughter of Llyr

The Second Branch of the Mabinogion introduces the Llyr dynasty and highlights the feats of arms of this line of mythical sovereigns.

Bran, one of the children of the god Llyr, proclaimed himself the master of storms, just like his brother Manawydan. A giant without fear, Bran roamed vast lands and opposed the Irish. He had a sister called Branwen, a very beautiful young woman who lived in the heart of Harlech in Wales.

One day, the King of Ireland, Matholwch, while visiting Wales, fell in love with the beautiful Branwen and asked Bran for her hand in marriage. The council met to deliberate and finally gave their approval. One of their counsellors, Evnissyen, was, however, not consulted and was very bitter. Terribly upset, he decided to take his revenge on the Irish who were escorting Matholwch, and mutilated their horses. War only just managed to be averted and the Welsh had to offer piles of gold and silver and a magic cauldron to appease the wrath of the King of Ireland.

So Matholwch and Branwen reached Ireland. Their happiness was, however, short-lived because the story of the mutilated horses spread throughout the country and incited the proud population of Eire against poor Branwen. She was soon reduced to occupying the kitchens of the royal palace.

Humiliated and like a prisoner in her own home, she managed to warn her brother with the help of a small starling which she had tamed. Bran thus decided to gather his army and attack Ireland. Since he was a giant, he was unable to board any vessel and had to make a ford across the sea. Bran stretched out between the two shores to allow his army to pass over his body to Ireland. It was in this fashion that his troops invaded Ireland. The battle was hard and for a long time the outcome was uncertain. Despite enormous losses, the Welsh were finally victorious and returned to the castle of King Matholwch to celebrate their victory. Some wild Irish warriors had hidden in bags hanging along the pillars of the rooms of the castle. Evnissyen was suspicious and demanded to know what the large bags contained. He was told that they contained wheat and flour. Evnissyen felt each of the bags and throttled the warriors inside them. Despite this incident, a celebration was organised to seal the reconciliation between the Irish and the Welsh. During the feast, Evnissyen, opposed to peace, seized Gwern, the son of Branwen and Matholwch. In a fit of rage, he threw him into the flames.

So it was that the war recommenced. The Irish were close to beating their adversaries thanks to their magic cauldron, which brought back to life the warriors killed in battle. But Evnissyen, as tenacious as ever, managed to get into the cauldron and make it burst into pieces. So the Welsh took the victory but Evnissyen perished in the battle. Bran, mortally wounded, asked for his head to be cut off. The precious relic was taken to London where it was decided to bury it under the white hill with the head turned towards Europe, in order to protect the island from invaders. As for Branwen, she returned to Wales, where she died of a broken heart.

The spell of the kingdom of Dyfed

The Third Branch of the Mabinogion tells of the deeds of valour of the brother of Branwen and Bran, Manawydan Mac Llyr. We know that, upon the death of Pwyll, he married Rhiannon. One day, when they were walking with Pryderi and his wife, Manawydan and Rhiannon were enveloped in an enchanted fog that covered the unhappy kingdom of Dyfed. Once the fog had disappeared, all they could do was to view the sad desolation of their country in which all activity had ceased. Manawydan and Pryderi left for England, where they decided to settle. They were skilled craftsmen and did wonderful work with leather, thus incurring the wrath of the guildsmen, who were jealous of their dexterity. Driven out of England, Manawydan and Pryderi returned to Wales.

Shortly afterwards, whilst hunting a strange white boar, Pryderi penetrated an unknown castle at the end of a dense forest. He decided to take refreshment there at the source of a magic fountain but he became paralysed, the victim of a spell. His mother, Rhiannon, who managed to find him, met the same fate. Manawydan, left to his own devices and deprived of his dogs, decided that to survive he would grow wheat and work on the land. His fields extended as far as the eye could see. Alas, hoards of mice ravaged his plantations just before harvest, destroying all of his work in just a few nights. Manawydan managed to capture one of the little rodents and, impatient to take his revenge, ordered that it be hung. The mouse, however, was pregnant and many were those that demanded a pardon for the unfortunate rodent. Manawydan finally bowed to the entreaties of a bishop but, in exchange, asked him to release Pryderi and Rhiannon and to lift the spell on the kingdom of Dyfed.

The bishop was none other than Llwyd, a magician friend of Gwawl, the former admirer of Rhiannon, whom Manawydan had replaced in the affections of the beautiful woman. Llwyd had wanted to avenge his unfortunate companion and thus had desolated the lands over which Manawydan reigned. The mouse was freed and the spell was immediately lifted.

Math, King of Gwyned, Lleu and Blodeuedd

The Fourth Branch of the Mabinogion concerns the dynasty of the children of Don, of which the principal protagonists went by the names of Math, Gwydion, Arianrhod and Lleu (or Llew).

The king of Gwyned, Math, who also had formidable talents as a magician, could only sleep if his feet were resting on the lap of a young virgin.

Following pages

The Orkney Isles Ring of Brogdar, Scotland

She was seduced by her nephews, Gilfaethwy and Gwydion, and Math decided to punish them by changing them into animals. Math then undertook to find a replacement for the fallen virgin and considered Arianrhod. Unfortunately for him, she was already pregnant and would soon give birth to two sons, Dylan and Lleu. Arianrhod wanted to keep these children forever and deprived Lleu of his name, weapons and a woman. As soon as he was born, Dylan escaped the arms of his mother by diving into the sea. After he had disappeared, the oceans mourned his passing with roaring waves. As regards Lleu, he was able to find an ally in Gwydion.

Gwydion and the magician Math, now reconciled, decided to raise the young Lleu and obtained for him Blodeuedd ("born of flowers"), the most beautiful of young women. His mother Arianrhod had, in fact, forbidden him to marry a human woman. Other spells were cast upon poor Lleu, who gained much comfort from Blodeuedd. The young couple's happiness was, however, to be short-lived for Blodeuedd fell in love with Goronwy, Lord of Penlyn. They decided to assassinate Lleu but their plot failed. Lleu ("the brilliant man with the skilful hands") was merely injured and, assuming the form of an eagle, managed to take to the skies and escape. Gwydion returned Lleu to his human form and severely punished the unfaithful Blodeuedd by changing her into an owl.

The legendary exploits of Kulhwch

This story recounting the heroic adventures of Kulhwch is linked to the story of King Arthur but is undoubtedly the older version.

The young Kulhwch had to overcome a spell cast by his stepmother, who was married to the horseman Cildydd. He could only marry if he seduced Olwen, the daughter of the giant Yspaddaden. This hardly seemed to him to be a formidable fate until Kulhwch fell madly in love with the gracious Olwen. The giant, who like the Irish Balor only had one eye, did not approve and imposed a series of impossible tests on the gallant knight in an attempt to prevent the union. Kulhwch made his way to the court of King Arthur, where he found some companions. He had good need of them because the deeds of valour that he had to accomplish presented a real challenge: there were nearly forty almost impossible tasks to be performed, without doubt one of the longest

quests of universal mythology. Among other tasks, Kulhwch had to catch the magic birds of Rhiannon; clear a forest and work and manage the land within a single day; bring a magic cauldron to the giant; steal the crown of an underwater king; tame a wild dog; break in a magic horse; and, the hardest task of all, hunt a ferocious boar, Twrch Trwyth, who carried a comb, a razor and some scissors between his ears. This enormous pig was none less than a king who had been punished by God for his sins.

For this last task, Kulhwch obtained the help of King Arthur himself and of Mabon, son of the goddess Modron. First of all, he had to go in search of Mabon and free him, for he was being held prisoner at Gloucester castle. The knights were led to Mabon's gaol by the magic salmon of Llynn Llaw. Kulhwch and his companions then set out on their long journey and pursued the magic boar across Wales, Cornwall and Ireland. Thanks to his riding and hunting talents, Mabon was able to seize the precious objects which Twrch Trwyth was carrying and give them to Kulhwch.

Once the knight had achieved his quest, he made his way to the terrible Yspaddaden and the giant had to consent to the union of the two young lovers.

The bard Taliesin

According to Welsh mythology, Taliesin was the first to acquire the gift of prophecy. At the time, he was called Gwyon Bach and was a domestic servant at the home of Keridwen. Having drunk three drops of the magic elixir from the cauldron of knowledge belonging to the witch Keridwen, he gained access to all the secrets of the past, the present and the future. The witch, however, furious that he had taken her potion, set out in pursuit of Gwyon Bach and, after many adventures, finally caught him. She swallowed him in the form of a grain of wheat and fell pregnant shortly afterwards. Keridwen then gave birth to a boy, whom she abandoned to the sea. The child was recovered and protected. He was named Taliesin ("beautiful seafront") and he became the most famous of the Welsh bards. In the 17th century, Geoffrey of Monmouth integrated him into the cycle of the legends of King Arthur and featured him in the *History of the Kings of Britain* beside Merlin the magician and Morgan the fairy.

It does seem that a Taliesin did actually exist in the 6th century and some of his texts written in ancient

Welsh have even been found. Tradition, however, has subsequently attributed other texts to Taliesin which he could not have written since they date from the 7th and 8th centuries.

Les Dépouilles D'Anwynn, particularly, figures among the most beautiful poems of Welsh literature, relating how Arthur seized a magic cauldron, a foreshadowing of the Holy Grail.

The Legend of King Arthur and the Quest for the Holy Grail

Moulded from ancient Celtic traditions, the Legend of King Arthur (Artus in medieval French) was at its most popular during the Middle Ages, when the stories of the "Matter of Britain" by Geoffrey of Monmouth or by Chrétien de Troyes spread throughout a large part of Western Europe. Large parts from the Bible were also added to the originally Celtic-inspired story.

Historically, Arthur never enjoyed the important role assigned to him by legend. He was originally a warlord who, accompanied by his fiana, was constantly waging war and hiring out his services to kings. In the 6th century AD, he led the British resistance against the Saxon invasion. Arthur became very popular in Great Britain; his exploits were embellished and incorporated into national mythology. The legend created a conquering and powerful king, surrounded by gallant companions known as the Knights of the Round Table. Acquiring a mythological dimension, the character of Arthur incorporated all the virtues of the Celtic universe and radiated its influence over all the Briton lands of Cornwall, Wales, Scotland, Ireland and Armorica.

In 1135, Geoffrey of Monmouth published his History of the *Kings of Britain* in Latin. The myth of Arthur was faithfully rewritten: a son of the king, Uther Pendragon, and of Igraine, the young Arthur educated by the wizard Myrddin (Merlin) became king at the age of fifteen and opposed the Saxons. This work inspired the Anglo-Norman Robert Wace, canon of Bayeux, who provided a liberal translation in his Roman de Brut (1155), undoubtedly at the instigation of Queen Eleanor of Aquitaine. As Queen of France and later of England, she supported artists and writers. She married Henry Plantagenet, Count of Anjou and Duke of Normandy, who became King of England in 1154. Eleanor surrounded herself with a brilliant court, where courtly literature flourished.

These stories told the French of the great feats of Arthur and his refined court. The court storytellers exploited the subject to the full. Several years previously, some epic poems had already described some of the major episodes influenced by Christianity. Certain stories, such as Huon of Bordeaux, would show the influence of Breton literature, particularly in the important part devoted to marvellous occurrences. In the last text, the enchanter Oberon, or Auberon, reveals his powers. This is undoubtedly the story of the "King of the Elves" from German legend, which appears again in Shakespeare's A Midsummer Night's Dream, the work of Christoph Martin Wieland and in the opera of Carl Maria von Weber.

Tristan and Isolde

The saga of Tristan and Isolde hailed from the same source. In the 7th century, Béroul and Thomas of England each published a Tristan of which quite important fragments have been preserved. The legend tells of the everlasting love that united Tristan and Isolde, imposing itself upon them, despite their efforts to free themselves.

Nephew of King Mark of Cornwall, Tristan received the education of a perfect knight. An accomplished horseman, he quickly became an excellent hunter. He also knew how to play the harp and handle weapons. His first exploit consisted of winning a duel against the Irish giant Morholt, who had come to demand a tribute of three hundred girls and three hundred boys at the court of King Mark. Tristan floored the giant but he was so badly injured that he preferred to take to the sea on a frail vessel. Reaching the coast of Ireland, he was taken in and looked after by the Queen of Ireland, sister of Morholt, and her daughter, the sweet Isolde. Frightened of being recognised as the murderer of Morholt, Tristan quickly returned to Cornwall. There, King Mark, pressured by his barons, decided to take a wife.

Preferring to make Tristan his successor, the King was in no rush to marry and so chose to marry the woman with a hair of gold, brought by the wind in the morning, certain that no-one would find her.

Tristan recognised the hair which belonged to fair Isolde and, wishing to prove his disinterest, started out at once to look for the beautiful woman with the hair of gold.

Arriving in Ireland, Tristan delivered the kingdom from a terrible dragon but remained paralysed because he had been touched by the poisoned tongue of the monster. Isolde found him unconscious and brought him back to life, hoping to be united with the handsome knight since she was promised to he who triumphed over the dragon.

Alas, the beautiful woman with the golden hair was soon to discover that her hero was also the murderer of her uncle Morholt. Isolde pardoned Tristan, however, but she was cruelly disappointed when she realised that he wished her hand for his uncle, King Mark of Cornwall.

During the return voyage, they accidentally drank a magic potion of eternal love. From that point onward, nothing could stand in the way of their passion. After many adventures, the lovers, pursued by King Mark, finally perished. Upon learning their secret, the King decided to bury them in two neighbouring tombs at the heart of a deep forest.

There, the brambles grew and intertwined in such a way that the two lovers found themselves connected as never before. So it was that Tristan and Isolde remained united beyond death.

Inspired by the spirit of the legend, Richard Wagner composed an admirable musical drama in three acts entitled *Tristan and Isolde* (1865) and, at the end of 19th century, the medievalist Jospeh Bédier undertook the rewriting of the legend and in 1900 published le *Roman de Tristan et Iseult*, adding to the literary value of the work.

A European legend

Following the Roman de Brut by Robert Wace, in which he included the essential elements of the tale (the Round Table and the Sword of Excalibur), the legend of King Arthur grew from adaptation to adaptation, crossing the whole of Europe, from Provence to the Germanic countries.

Chrétien de Troyes is, without doubt, the writer who endowed the legend of King Arthur with noble qualities. He wrote five books on the subject:

Eric et Enide (Eric and Enide), Cligès, Lancelot (Lancelot or the Knight of the Cart), Yvain ou le Chevalier au lion (Yvain or the Knight with the Lion) and Perceval ou le Conte du Graal (Perceval or the Story of the Grail).

In the 13th century, the novels written in verse from the previous century were adapted into prose and the works of Chrétien de Troyes were reworked by anonymous authors who specifically developed the theme of the Holy Grail, affirming its sense of mystery. A veritable cycle was compiled under the name of *Lancelot en prose: l'Estoire del Saint- Graal (The Story of the Holy Grail), l'Estoire de Merlin l'Enchanteur (The Story of Merlin the Enchanter), le Livre de Lancelot du Lac (The Book of Lancelot of the Lake), la Queste del Saint Graal (The Quest of the Holy Grail)* and *la Mort de Roi Artu (The Death of King Arthur).*

In the 15th century, Sir Thomas Malory was inspired by the texts, notably the French ones, to compose his *Le Morte D'Arthur* thus allowing British literature to rediscover the Arthurian cycle.

Arthur and the Knights of the Round Table

These stories differ noticeably from one version to another. Originally, the Celtic aspects were more important and Arthur was similar to Finn McCool of the Fenian myths. The importance of the Arthur-Merlin duo represented the king-druid duality upon which Celtic society was based. This is highlighted noticeably by Jean Markale in his books. Subsequently, under the influence of both Christianity and feudal society, the orientation of the cycle changed, new characters appeared and the mystical aspect became more important, particularly with the Quest for the Holy Grail.

Historic quests, fabulous voyages, tournaments, duels, assaults against dragons etc. – the knights had to undergo a veritable initiation process, which took them far away from Camelot. The names of the main protagonists apart from Arthur and Merlin were the fairy Vivien; Guinevere; Gawain; Lancelot; the fairy Morgan; Kay, the seneschal of Arthur, who proved a formidable warrior; Bedivere the one-armed warrior; the knight Geraint (Eric in the story of Chrétien de Troyes); Yvain; Calogrenant; Galahad; Perceval and Peredur.

Upon the death of Uther Pendragon, the Knights of the Round Table gathered at Tintagel castle to designate a successor to the late King. Unable to reach agreement, they requested the counsel of Merlin. The enchanter replied that their next king would be the one who managed to extract the magic sword set in the rock of a clearing.

Tristan takes an oath after having been made a Knight of the Round Table

Perhaps inspired by the Irish myth of Diarmaid and Grainne, the legend of Tristan and Isolde remains one of the favourite subjects of western literature. Closely linked to the story of King Arthur, it has been the inspiration for many works: the story of Tristan by the Anglo-Norman Thomas, Tristan by Béroul from the 12th century, Tristan ménéstrel by Gerbert de Montreuil from the 13th century, Tristan and Isolde by Gottfried de Strasbourg from the 13th century, le Tristan en prose from the 13th century etc. In the opera by Richard Wagner composed in 1865, Tristan became one of the Romantic heroes par excellence, not submitting to his fate but aspiring to a liberating death. In the cinema, Tristan was interpreted by Jean Marais in l'Eternal Retour (1943), a modern version of the myth showcasing the talent of Jean Delannoy and Jean Cocteau.

This task was attempted by many knights but always in vain. During a tournament, Arthur succeeded in removing the sword and was immediately designated the successor to Uther Pendragon.

Arthur soon realised that this decision was not universally welcomed by the knights surrounding him and had to confront several of them in duels. One day, when fighting one of his adversaries, his sword broke. Arthur obtained the help of Merlin, who plunged the aggressive knight into a deep sleep. Still deprived of his sword, however, Arthur fell into a deep depression. While the unarmed sovereign was walking on the banks of a big lake, he was suddenly surprised to see a hand emerging from the water holding a resplendent sword. It was the Lady of the Lake, the fairy Vivien who had come to comfort Arthur and return the famous Excalibur, "the violent thunder", the magic sword from the other world.

Thanks to his new weapon, Arthur recovered his sovereignty and affirmed his supremacy over the kingdom. Shortly afterwards, he married Guinevere. During the ceremony, the enchanter Merlin offered Arthur the fabulous Round Table, designed to prevent all quarrels of precedence among the knights.

Merlin the Enchanter

The origins of Merlin seem obscure seeing as he was the child of a demon. Having inherited a large part of the demon's powers, the young Merlin proved his natural gifts very early on by throwing light upon many inexplicable mysteries. When King Vortigern tried to build a castle which kept collapsing, Merlin demonstrated that this was hardly surprising since two gigantic dragons were fighting every night on the foundations of the fortress. He also predicted that the red dragon, representing the Saxons, would be victorious over the white dragon, representing the Britons. Appointed a seer by King Uther, he was present at the very conception of the Arthur story. Despite his wisdom, Merlin fell in love with the fairy Vivien, who bewitched him and stole some of his powers.

It was also Merlin who introduced to the castle of Camelot the famous Round Table, which was large enough to seat one hundred knights. For the whole of his long reign, Arthur had a clever counsellor and faithful ally. Merlin's disappearance remained an enigma for many. One day, he was assisting at the Council of Knights and accidentally took the place which only Galahad was allowed to occupy, being the only one to have contemplated the Grail. Merlin disappeared underground never to return.

The Knight Gawain

Nephew of the king, the Knight Gawain was definitely one of the most "courteous" of Arthur's companions and even though he failed in his quest for the Grail, he was always unfailingly chivalrous. French tradition presents him as one of the possessors of the last flower of chivalry but prefers his companion Lancelot, who was his rival. The British versions present him as more of a combatant, as the following story illustrates.

One evening, as the knights were gathered around the king, a green giant penetrated the council chamber in the castle of Camelot and attacked the assembly. Gawain took up the challenge and cut the throat of the troublemaker. But to his great surprise, the giant seemed unaffected! He simply picked up his head and, addressing Gawain, demanded a duel with hatchets to take place one year later, next to the green chapel.

On the appointed date, Gawain set out for the thick forest where the duel was to take place. Some way from his destination, he made a stop at the dwelling of a lord and met a very beautiful woman, the wife of his host. Although seduced by the apparition, Gawain did, however, manage to reject her advances but the noble knight finally accepted a scarf of green silk from his hostess, a sign that he was not impervious to her charm.

When he came face to face with his terrible adversary, Gawain was surprised to discover that the green giant was none other than the lord who had welcomed him. The shock was brutal. The giant hurled his hatchet at Gawain three times; the first two times the weapon just brushed the neck of the knight but, at the last attempt, his neck was injured and bled. This was obviously the giant's attempt to make him understand that he had fallen short in accepting the scarf from his beautiful hostess. But since he had not committed the irreparable sin of betraying his host, his throat was not cut. To remind him of his mistake, Gawain always kept the precious scarf, which had, after all, protected him from a worse fate.

Dommiet la veille de la penthe
couste q le Roy artus deuoit tenir
court plenie anuia vne damoiselle q demandoit
lacelot de lac et cultelin monstra claime.
sen alla apres elle r elle le mena en
vne abbaye ou estoit galaad son filz [et]

Dit le compte
que la veille de
sa penthecoste
q celle trait
assemblee fu fai
te de dame kanne
loth se la fem

anecquit luy Boort de isannes r pho
quel lequel Il fist cela Et landemain
lermitte que na galaad a la court du Roy
artus et le fist assoir au sixte pillier
ou gl homme ne sestoit asse et la Jls
trouuerent le nom de galaad en escript

Ces seigneurs
cheuuliers
Assez y peu
sier veoir ho
neur et prie
z cheualeu
et hantesse

Lancelot of the Lake

To begin with, Merlin was opposed to the plan to unite Arthur and Guinevere in marriage, because he could not ignore the tender feelings that Guinevere had for Lancelot, the most handsome and valiant of the Knights of the Round Table. It is to be noted here that the character of Lancelot never appeared in the Welsh legends and that he was introduced into the cycle by Chrétien de Troyes.

He is called Lancelot of the Lake because the fairy Vivien, his protector, plunged him into a pool when he was a child. He took many benefits from this. Arriving at the court of King Arthur, the gallant knight fell in love with Queen Guinevere and performed a thousand deeds of valour, as much for her as for King Arthur. For many years, Lancelot must have been champing at the bit, for Guinevere rejected his advances but finally they became lovers. The choice between passion and service to the king was not easy because Lancelot was neither a liar nor a rogue. The misfortune of Arthur had far-reaching consequences and real problems ensued: the unity of the Knights of the Round Table was broken. Lancelot left for Armorica with Arthur pursuing him and assaulting his Breton fortress. Arthur is said to have lifted the siege upon learning that his nephew Mordred, brandishing the banner of revolt, had seized Camelot, the city castle of the Knights of the Round Table. On returning to England, King Arthur assembled his knights to confront Mordred's troops in a fratricidal combat. The two armies went to battle at Camlann on Salisbury plain, not far from the megalithic site of Stonehenge, and British knighthood fell into the fray. This legendary episode seems to correspond to the hard battles in 541 fought between the island Britons and the Saxons historically marking the triumph of the Angles and the Saxons.

Fatally wounded, Arthur asked to be taken from the field of battle and begged one of his faithful companions, the one-armed Bedivere, to take care of Excalibur. When Bedivere threw the magic sword into the lake at the request of the dying king, the fairy Vivien seized it in flight, thus retrieving her property. Arthur then reached Avalon on an enchanted barge guided by the fairies. There he could rest peacefully, not dead but sleeping, watched over by the fairy Morgan surrounded by her nine sisters. When the time came, Arthur would awake to re-establish his sovereignty over a new Celtic kingdom.

Lancelot

A passionate knight, valiant warrior, hero without fear but not without reproach, Lancelot is the most famous of the knights of King Arthur. Originally from Armorica, the character was incorporated into the legend by Chrétien de Troyes at the beginning of the 12th century. It was the fairy Vivien, the famous "Lady of the Lake", who taught him the duties of a knight: "None of the assembled knights attracted more attention or were more celebrated than Lancelot of the Lake. For many years, Lancelot was the honour of the court of King Arthur. More gracious and more daring than any of the others, he was recognised everywhere as the finest knight in the world. There was a charming mystique about this character. The origins of his race went so far back that all that is known are fables: he was raised by the water fairies in an enchanted palace and his name, Lancelot of the Lake, was a reminder of this poetic childhood." (La Queste du Graal, adaptation of Albert Pauphilet, 1923).

Following pages
Isle of Lewis: Callanish Stones

This circle of the raised stones of Callanish is located on the Isle of Lewis, the largest of the Hebrides in Scotland.

This last image is also quite reminiscent of the Germanic legend of the famous Frederick I Barbarossa, who was killed in a crusade in 1190 and who slept an enchanted sleep under the mountain crowned with the ruins of castle Kyffhäuser in Thuringia, before returning to take his place at the head of a restored empire.

The Quest for the Grail

The Holy Grail of medieval literature is the descendent of the magic cauldrons of Celtic mythology: cauldrons of abundance and revival but also a symbol of sovereignty. According to Arthurian legend, it was the cup served to Christ at the Last Supper, in which Joseph of Arimathea collected the blood of Christ during the crucifixion. This vessel was passed down through Joseph and his descendants but it is not known how it left Palestine. When the Knights of the Round Table decided to embark on the Quest for the Holy Grail, Arthur was saddened because he feared that the best of his knights would disappear on this noble mission. To succeed in this epic not only required exceptional physical attributes but, above all, intense spiritual qualities bordering on perfection. Many of the knights failed. Gawain undoubtedly did not have the required humility; Lancelot came close to succeeding, even reaching the castle of Carbonek which housed the Grail, but he could not enter because he had sinned too much. The naïve purity of the young Perceval would have permitted him to reach the Grail but he lacked the courage. Having become a Knight of the Round Table, Perceval was one day welcomed to the court of the Fisher King. There he witnessed a strange procession: A man lead the way brandishing a blood-covered spear; then came torches followed by two young women, one carrying a sparkling vase of precious stones and the other a silver plate. Speechless with admiration, Perceval did not dare to question his host as to the significance of these marvels and lost his only chance to approach the Grail. It was finally Galahad, the son of Lancelot, who succeeded with the Grail. He was accompanied by the knights Perceval and Bohort but only Galahad was able to behold it. When he raised the Grail in his hands, the young knight knew the ecstasy which symbolised mystical happiness. His soul escaped his body and was brought to heaven by the angels. In response to the wish of Joseph of Arimathea, Galahad drank a sip from the sacred cup and received the holy sacrament which assured eternal spiritual life.

In the 13th century, the German poet Wolfram von Eschenbach wrote a beautiful version of the myth in *Parzival*, which was the inspiration for the *Parsifal* of Richard Wagner.

Legends and Romanticism

The Arthurian cycle and Celtic mythology influenced the Romantic movement. The word *roman*, which is at the origin of the adjective romantic, designates stories written, not in Latin, but in a romance language, particularly the collection of texts of the "Matter of Britain".

In Europe at the end of the 18th century, the Middle Ages were rediscovered. In 1760, James McPherson published the poems of the bard Ossian while William Blake laid the foundations for English Romanticism, the movement in which the poets Wordsworth, Coleridge, Shelley, Keats and Byron would be the leadings authors.

Sir Walter Scott, author of many heroic novels (*Waverley*, 1814; *Ivanhoe*, 1819; *Quentin Durward*, 1823) returned Scottish myths and chivalry to a place of honour throughout Europe. Germaine de Staël highlighted this in her own fashion in *De la littérature* (1800): "The English poets who have succeeded the Scottish bards… have retained the imagination of the North…, which takes to the future and to another world, the soul weary of its destiny. The imagination of the men of the North soars beyond this earth whose confines they inhabit; it soars beyond the clouds which border their horizons and seems to represent the obscure passage of life to eternity."

With the Napoleonic Wars, the enthusiasm for the French Revolution was soon replaced by the exultation of national virtues, Christian mysticism and a return to the mythical images of primitive stories and legends. Reacting against the rationalism of the Enlightenment, Johann Herder initiated the *Sturm und Drang* ("storm and stress") movement, by advocating a "natural poetry", drawing its inspiration from the national soul. His Stimmen der *Völker in Liedern* (1788), a collection of folk songs, marks the climax of *Sturm und Drang* and also the beginning of German Romanticism. Countless collections of national myths, legends and fairy tales

The Dream of Ossian

Nordic myth: Ossian and the ancient Scottish bards. In the 19th century, Romantic Europe developed a passion for the legendary figure brought back to life by the poet James McPherson. According to Irish tradition, Ossian, son of Finn, was named Oisin (little fawn) and accomplished many exploits. Ernest Renan imagined the conversations which the bard held with Saint Patrick in Essais de morale et de critique (Moral and Critical Essays): "Although my memory weakens and worry eats at my heart, I wish to continue to sing the stories of the past and to live from the ancient glory. Now I am old, my life is slipping away and all my joys disappearing. My hand can no longer hold the sword, nor my arm handle the spear..." Drawing by Jean-Auguste-Dominique Ingres, about 1812.

were written, such as *Des Knaben Wunderhorn* (1805-08) by Achim von Arnim and Clemens Brentano; *Kinder und Hausmärchen* (1812-14) by the brothers Jakob and Wilhelm Grimm; and *Die teutschen Volksbücher* (1805-08) by Johann von Görres.Prior to this, Johann Wolfgang Goethe's Die Leiden des Jungen Werther (The Sorrows of Young Werther, 1774) and Friedrich Schiller's *Die Räuber* (The Robbers, 1782) had already made a profound effect on the concept of consciousness and the individual, as can be traced in German poetry from Novalis and Jean-Paul to the more political Heine.

Lyrical Romanticism later evolved into fantastic poetry. In France, following Victor Hugo with *la Légende des siècles* (Legend of the Centuries), Charles Nodier, notably the author of *Trilby* or le *Lutin d'Argail* (1822) (The Elf of Argail) and of la *Fée aux miettes* (1832), Aloysius Bertrand, Maurice de Guérin and Gérard de Nerval illustrated this trend.

The Lord of the Rings

In the 20th century, fantasy literature, cinema, cartoons (notably with the character of Prince Vaillant, created in the United States in 1937) adopted Celtic myths and made them popular.

The works of the Briton John Ronald Reuel Tolkien, translated throughout the world, clearly illustrate this tendency. His first book, *The Hobbit* (1937) was written for children, but it was principally in the *Lord of the Rings* trilogy (1954-56) that his imaginative talent came to the fore. Borrowing from both Nordic mythology and the medieval universe, Tolkien retraces the long struggle for possession of the magic rings. A seasoned medievalist – he was notably the author of *A Middle English Vocabulary* (1922) and a study on *Gawain the Green Knight* (1925) – Tolkien also gave us the eternal conflict between the forces of light (the land of Numenor) and the forces of darkness (the land of Mordor). It is not very difficult to explain this emergence of fantasy in our present-day societies. As early as the 19th century, Charles Nodier had the following diagnosis: "The appearance of fables recommences at the moment in which ends the influence of real or perceived truths which lend a little soul to the worn mechanism of civilisation. It is this which has rendered fantasy so popular in France over the last few years and which provides the only essential literature of the age of decadence and the period of transition in which we find ourselves."

Vivien and Merlin

"One day, I went into the forest with my love, I fell asleep at the foot of a thorn bush, my head in her lap; she raised herself gracefully and made a circle around the bush with her veil; and when I awoke, I found myself upon a magnificent bed in the most beautiful and closed chamber I had ever seen" (Lancelot in prose).

Photography by Julia Margaret Cameron (1815-79).

GERMANIC MYTHOLOGY

The Germanic Peoples

The Germanic peoples originally occupied a vast domain in the centre and the north of Europe, comprising a territory delimited by the Rhine, the Danube and the Vistula; the Baltic islands and a large part of Scandinavia. Warriors and peasants, the Germanic peoples lived in tribes under the authority of warlords. They were often on the move, looking for fertile ground, but were not nomads. The society was organised in a hierarchical fashion around a nobility of landowners: military chiefs were elected from among them. Accomplished riders, they crossed Europe armed with iron swords. Their chariots have been found in many tombs and under burial mounds, comparable to those of the Celts, from Champagne to Bohemia and up to the south of what today is Poland. Like the Greeks, the Latins, the Celts and the Slavs, and also the Iranians and the Indians, they belong to the great Indo-European family.

The rough warriors

The Teutons, Cimbri, Goths, Visigoths, Ostrogoths, Vandals, Burgundians, Franks, Friesians, Lombards (or Longobars), Alamans, Marcomanni, Suevi, Saxons, Angles and Jutes were all Germanic peoples and, although there was no political unity governing them, the essential common factor was the language, which is no longer known to us in its original form. Large in number, these tribes travelled great distances across Europe but some of them experienced a rapid decline. André Maurois gives us some useful information on this topic: "Tacitus was the first to state clearly that the Germanic people had a point of unity. He distinguished between three groups of tribes: the Ingvaeones, the Herminones and the Istvaeones, who worshipped different gods. According to Tacitus, however, all had grey and blue eyes and red hair; all of them, when fighting, sang a chorus to enflame their courage. In fact, Tacitus' distinctions were more religious than tribal. His Ingvaeones were the Cimbri who lived on the shores of the North Sea and, like the Teutons and the Vandals, were often driven inland by frequent flooding. There were also the Jutes, the Angles and the Friesians. Tacitus' Herminones were the Suevi, the first inhabitants of what would become Lower Austria, Moravia and Bohemia. The Istvaeones were the Cherusci, the Batavians and the Sugameri who lived on the banks of the Rhine, the Lippe, the Ruhr and the Main."

The Germanic peoples lived from agriculture and stock breeding. They knew how to cultivate, mill wheat and work the soil using rudimentary ploughs pulled by oxen. These were the rough warriors who had practiced metallurgy techniques since the 4th century BC. Their arms were fearsome: large iron swords, long spears, javelins, daggers, battle axes, sabres (short blades), breastplates, round shields and helmets similar to those of the Celtic soldiers. During battles, they worshipped Tyr, the god of war. Not only were the Germanic peoples remarkable warriors but they also established a judicial system based on their customs. One of the principles of this summary legislation remained intangible: The guilty party could turn over a new leaf and redeem himself if the victim or their family agreed to forego vengeance. A scale of punishments was carefully established according to the severity of the crimes committed. As early as the 2nd century AD, several Germanic peoples developed a system of writing, probably inspired by the Latin alphabet but also similar to the Gaelic oghams: the runic script with evident symbolic value. More than a real means of communication, the runes were primarily used for practicing magic.

The soul of the forest

Priestesses of the forest in a procession to pay homage to some nourishing deity.

Oil on wood, by Maxence Edgar (1871-1954), musée des Beaux Arts, Nantes. A.D.A.G.P.

These signs which covered commemorative stones, arms and jewellery, had a prophetic power. They actually constituted the first manifestations of poetic genius as shown by Renauld-Krantz in his *Anthologie de la poésie nordique ancienne* (1964).

Germanic peoples and Romans: often complex relations

Very early on, trade was organised with the Mediterranean world and the Romans but conflicts escalated rapidly. From the 2nd century BC, Teutons and Cimbri reached southern Gaul and the western Alps but were destroyed by the Romans. In the year 102 BC, Marius, in the area of Aix-en-Provence, near the Saint-Victoire mountain, broke the assault of the Teuton army and took close to three hundred thousand prisoners. The following year, the Cimbri suffered a similar fate in the North of Italy. A century later, in the year 9 AD, under Augustus, the Germanic chief Arminius (Hermann) defeated the Roman legions of Varus in the Teutoburg forest, in this way marking the limits of Roman power to the East of the Rhine and prefiguring the autonomous evolution of Germania. Many monuments have been erected in the honour of Hermann, considered a national hero, particularly the one in the Teutoburg forest, dating from 1875. Heinrich von Kleist pays homage to Hermann in *Die Hermannsschlacht* (1808).

The Germanic peoples progressively moved towards the west and the south, driving back or assimilating the Celtic populations and spreading throughout a large part of Europe. Saxons, Alamans and Franks were living in Germania. At the frontiers of the Roman Empire, they exerted ever more pressure, profiting from the decline of Rome to extend their influence. In Bohemia and Moravia, it was the Marcomanni; on the banks of the Danube, the Vandals. The Lombards traversed Sicily and crossed the Danube. In the 3rd century, the great mass of Burgundians emigrated westwards and settled on the Main. To the east, the Gepidae and the Goths, coming from the Baltic, settled in the Ukraine and southern Russia. Other tribes reached Scandinavia and were already mounting raids against Celtic Britain, where Roman influence was relatively superficial. The Romans often established cordial relations with their barbarian neighbours, installing them as "federates" at the frontiers of the empire and integrating them into their armed forces.

The mysterious charm of the Germanic forests

"In this period, plunged for us into a shadowy light where magic glows sparkle here and there, there are in these woods, among these rocks, these glens, only apparitions, visions, prodigious meetings, fiendish hunts, infernal castles, the noise of harps in the coppice, melodious songs sung by invisible songstresses and terrible roars of laughter from mysterious passers-by. The human heroes, almost as fantastic as the supernatural figures, Cunon of Sayn, Sibo of Lorch, the strong sword, Griso the heathen, Attich, Duke of Alsace, Thassilo, Duke of Bavaria, Anthyse, Duke of the Franks, Samo, King of Vendes were frightened in these breathtaking forests, searching and crying for their beautiful women, tall and svelte white princesses crowned with charming names such as Gela, Garlinde, Liba, Williswinde, Schonetta. All these adventurers, half plunged into the impossible and grimly clinging on to reality, came and went in the legends, lost towards evening in inextricable forests, breaking the brambles and the pines, like the Knight of Death of Albrecht Dürer, under the hooves of their horses..."

Victor Hugo, *The Rhine* (1842)

Following pages

Viking burial place on Groix island, Morbihan.

According to numerous sources, Tacitus in particular, the Germanic peoples were passionate about games and also used dice as divining tools, particularly before battles.

In the 5th century, the Germanic peoples were themselves driven back by the Huns, who came from the vast north of Siberia, penetrating the Roman Empire in force. The phenomenon of great migrations was amplified. The Visigoths invaded the Balkans, then a part of Italy and the south-west of Gaul. From there they took Spain. Franks, Vandals and Burgundians penetrated into Gaul. The Vandals crossed the Pyrenees and reached North Africa, while Italy was dominated by the Ostrogoths, then the Lombards. In 476, the last Roman emperor in the west was deposed by barbarian armies. This is a symbolic date marking the end of Antiquity. The Angles, Jutes and Saxons arrived in Britain and set up small autonomous kingdoms, pushing the native populations to the west of the island. The legendary figure of King Arthur symbolises the Celtic resistance, which was soon to be annihilated.

Roman law and Germanic customs

Contrary to the Celts, the Germanic peoples were able to impose their power long-term in the territories which they conquered. The relationships that they established with the populations living under Roman law varied from one region to another. In certain regions, in England or the north of Belgium, the Roman civilisation was swept away. Sometimes, however, where the Germanic settlers were fewer, they had to assimilate themselves or form communities separate from those of the natives. In Gaul, Frankish custom won over in the north, while Roman law was maintained in the south of the country. This division between countries with "customary law" and countries with "written law" was, however, not immutable and frontiers could evolve. While the heathen peoples, the Franks or the Saxons, for example, converted to Christianity fairly rapidly, other peoples, on the other hand, such as the Goths or the Vandals, converted to a heretical Christianity, Arianism, appearing more stubborn and offering organised resistance to the evangelism of Roman missionaries.

In the 6th century, Grégoire de Tours described the Frankish people, undoubtedly some of the least Romanized of the barbarians: "he does not know God; he constructs images of forests, water, birds, wild beasts and other elements; he makes a cult around them and offers sacrifices to them." Julius Caesar had already

A Viking vessel

As early as the end of the 8th century with the expansion of the peoples of the North, the Vikings (from vik: bay) and Scandinavia entered history. The appearance of the sail, linked with oars, on Danish ships, and the orientation techniques of the sailors enabled the Scandinavian navigators to reach the coastal archipelagos of Scotland, Ireland and Iceland. The Norwegians went even further and discovered Greenland (981), then around the year 1000, a country populated with an indigenous people, probably America. The Swedish took the routes to the east and reached the Caspian Sea and the Black Sea. On the western coasts of the European continent, it was mainly the Danes who landed on the shores of the Channel and the Atlantic coast. The discovery of several royal tombs in Norway has made it possible to uncover relatively well-preserved vessels, which have been reconstructed. These boats without deck cargo, ten to twenty metres (33-66 ft.) long and five metres (16ft) wide, were designed for both long crossings and rapid landings and could transport fifty to one hundred and fifty men. The prows of these vessels were sometimes decorated with heads of dragons (drakkars) or serpents (snäkkars).

highlighted the importance of the sun and moon cult to the Germanic peoples. It is, however, Tacitus, in his *De Germania*, who provides us with more precious information regarding this religion, as early as the 1st century AD, almost ten centuries before the most ancient Germanic sources.

Two essential factors relativise this contribution however: firstly, Tacitus was predominantly interested in the Germanic peoples of the west, those living on the banks of the Rhine and in the surrounding area, and ignored those who came from the north

and the east. Secondly, like Julius Caesar before him, with regard to Gallic gods, Tacitus understood Germanic beliefs from a Roman point of view and sometimes erroneously interpreted the information that he received.

Finally, the diversity of the peoples concerned complicates the task of historians: The Saxon gods were not those of the Vandals and the tribes of the Rhine did not worship the same deities as those of the Baltic islands. Medieval sources, essentially documents of ecclesiastical origin, contemporary to the

period when the Germanic peoples converted to Christianity, are not of the same value. Often lacking objectivity, most of these texts aimed to denigrate or repress the pagan beliefs of the primitive populations. Certain authors, however, such as the bishop of Clermont, Sidoine Apollinaire, in the 5th century, Grégoire de Tours and the Venerable Bede, in the 8th century, or Adam de Brême in the 11th century give us important indications, although they remain sketchy. There, as elsewhere, the spread of Christianity was accompanied by an eradication of the ancient beliefs.

the ancient beliefs took place. The most we have is a description from Adam of Brême, in the 11th century, of the temple of Uppsala. There is no proof that the strange rocks of the Extersteine (Teutoburg forest, Westphalia) and the small cave perched at the top of one of them are related to any form of sun worship. However, if some think that the relief of the 12th century sealed in the famous stone celebrates the victory of Christianity over paganism.

The texts of Edda

If our knowledge of the primitive religion of the Germanic peoples to the west and the south sometimes seems scant, the civilisation and mythology of the Germanic peoples established in Scandinavia are better known to us. Evangelized considerably later than the Germanic peoples of the south or the Goths, these pagan peoples long preserved a rough way of life where nature kept its prerogatives. In this way, they kept alive a certain number of practices and customs forgotten by their brothers in German and Anglo-Saxon countries.

The scholars who, from the 10th century, received this oral tradition and wrote down the mythological stories of the first ages, behaved in the same way as the Irish monks who safeguarded the Celtic legends by writing them down. These long epic collections, mostly anonymous, are called *Edda*. Even if these texts translate the beliefs relatively late, a substantial part of them relate to a period before the introduction of Christianity in Scandinavia.

The most important of these poems are entitled *The Battle of the Huns, The Lay of Volund, The Words of the High One* (Havamal), *Vafprudnismal, For Skìrnis* and *The Seeress' Prophecy* (Völuspa). In this last story, a prophetess sees the history of the world, from the origin of time and the coming of the gods until the final catastrophe. This source of undeniable literary richness provides very important information about the Germanic gods. Added to this are the sagas, epic songs of the Scandinavian skalds (poets) who, in the Middle Ages, retraced the feats and acts of the heroes of Germanic legend. There is also a similarity with Viking epics. Some of these texts such as *The Old Lay of Biarki* relate directly to episodes from the Viking period.

The runic stones

Runes go back to the 2nd century AD. A means of expression of the ancient Germanic peoples, with an undeniably magical character, there are many examples of runic writing in stone, notably in Scandinavia and Great Britain. The word rune comes from the ancient Scandinavian rûnar and the Gothic runa ("magic sign"). The most ancient runic tradition is that of Elder futhark, which had twenty four characters. Paradoxically, in the 9th century, that is to say at the dawn of the golden age of the Viking, the runic alphabet was simplified, changing from twenty-four to sixteen signs.

It is very rare that the incantations or magic chants have survived to the present day; the formulas said to be from Mersburg contain only a few verses.

Roman, Irish and German missionaries successively spread the Good Word and did their utmost to eradicate the pagan remnants of popular belief. The Germanic gods were exiled and the superstitions fiercely fought. Sometimes, the myths were collected and Christianised. Most of the Christian festivals correspond to the old pagan festivals and the names of the days of the week date back to the worship of the ancient Germanic gods. The Christian celebration of Christmas corresponds to the pagan festival of the winter solstice, Jul; the celebration of Ostara became Easter; the festival of the summer solstice became the celebration of Saint John the Baptist. Hardly any remains have been found of the sanctuaries where ceremonies and sacrifices of

Of considerable note are the poems of Sigvat Thordarson (11th century), Einar Skulason (12th century) and the writings of the Icelandic scholar Snorri Sturlusen who, in the 13th century, published an anthology of skaldic art. We should also mention the Latin manuscripts left by the Dane Saxo Grammaticus in the 13th century. Archaeology also attests to many types of magic and religious practices. The most ancient relic found remains the gold horn of Gallehus, discovered in the 17th century on the island of Seeland, in Denmark. This richly decorated religious object dates back to the 4th century. The gods Odin, Thor and Frey are represented on it, as are several animals. Also worth noting is the funeral inscription written in the runic alphabet and engraved on the stone of Tune, Norway, in the 5th century. Many other relics have been found: a commemorative stone from the 6th century from Sanda, Gotland, Sweden; 7th century treasure found in a funeral boat at Sutton Hoo, England; a sculpture in stone from the 8th century representing Odin on his eight-legged horse, discovered at Alskog, Gotland, Sweden; figurative stone from the 8th century showing the god Thor, discovered at Labro, Sweden; funeral boats from Oseberg, Norway, from the 9th century; runic stone from the 11th century, discovered at Altuna, Sweden; runic stone from Hanning, Denmark; not to mention the numerous pendants, broaches, seals, amulets in hammer form evoking the god Thor, shields, helmets and Viking weapons.

The origin of the World and the Birth of the Gods

Young were the years when Ymir made his settlement,
there was no sand nor sea nor cool waves;
earth was nowhere nor the sky above,
chaos yawned, grass was there nowhere.
From the south, Sun, companion of the moon,
threw her right hand round the edge of the heaven;
Sun did not know where her hall might be,
the stars did not know where their place might be,
the moon did not know what power he had.

(translation from *The Poetic Edda –*
A New Translation by Carolyne Larrington)

This Icelandic poem describes the first phase of the world in Germanic mythology: absolute despair. The historian Paul Hermann in his *German Mythology* (1898) draws a striking parallel between this text and the prayer of *Wessobrun*, a *pagan* Saxon poem "concerned with the beginnings of the earth and describing the obscurity of the original chaos."

I experienced this among the nation as the most
pleasant miracle,The earth was not, above heaven,
Was still tree (still stone) still mountain;
The (star) none still sun shone,
Still the moon shone, still the sea so glorious,
And when there was nothing from end or change,
There was the one almighty god,
Mildest men and some were with him
Glorious spirits. And God the Holy….
Almighty God, who created Heaven and Earth,
and who Has given so much good to men,
have mercy upon me
The true belief, the true will, wisdom and intelligence
and Strength to resist the Devil and avoid evil and do
your will.

Midgard, the middle-enclosure, and Ásgard, the citadel of the gods

At the beginning of time, there reigned a terrible cold night, an original chaos, a bottomless abyss. Then the fire of the south, Muspelsheim, collided with the ice of the north, a universe of fog called Niflheim and, from this terrifying meeting, came the birth of the elements. The void, the Ginnungagap, was filled. The ice melted giving birth to a giant, Ymir, and the nourishing cow, Audhumla. The sweat of the giant, during his sleep, gave birth to new giants. By licking the blocks of ice surrounding her, Audhumla freed Búri. He had a son Bor, who married Bestla, descendant of the giant Ymir. Their union produced three gods, Odin, Vili and Vé.

So the terrible struggle of the giants and the gods began. On one side, the "giants of the frost" and on the other, the sons of Bor. Odin and his two brothers killed their ancestor, the venerable giant Ymir. The rivers of blood that flooded from his body drowned all the descendants of the giant with the exception of Bergelmir and his wife, who saved themselves on a little boat.

The tree with crows

Axis of the world, the tree had a primordial importance in the pagan religions of the peoples of the north. Tree of indestructible life in the image of Yggdrasill, it could also reveal itself as one of the vectors of death, the origin of the expression totenbaum *(tree of death), which represented hollow trees where the dead were sometimes buried.*

"The dreams and enchantments are children of the fog" *(Charles Baudelaire).*

Caspar David Friedrich (1774 – 1840), musée du Louvre.

This couple managed to engender a new race of giants, ready for revenge and for new battles. Odin and his brothers lifted the gigantic cadaver of Ymir and used it to construct the land which they called Midgard (middle- enclosure), situated between the burning Muspelsheim and the icy Niflheim. Worms issued forth from the decaying body of Ymir and the gods immediately transformed them into dwarves, destined for an underground existence. The blood of the giant became the sea and his bones formed the mountains. His skull formed the canopy of heaven. The three gods then seized the sparks of fire escaping from Muspelsheim and created the sun, the moon and the stars. They regulated the tides and allowed the birth of the seasons. They also determined the succession of days and nights. Soon, vegetation spread over the earth. But their task was not yet finished because they created the first humans by giving life to two tree trunks: the ash for the man, and the elm for the woman.

People became established in Midgard, while the gods gathered in their citadel of the heavens, Ásgard. A giant bridge, Bilfröst, connected the two universes. Heimdall, the god of light, was appointed to guard the bridge, a highly strategic place as it was the only point of communication between the two worlds. Composed of fire, air and water, Bilfröst appeared as a superb rainbow. Midgard, the middle-enclosure, was surrounded by a vast ocean, where a monstrous serpent reigned, large enough to encircle the inhabited lands with its coil. Below Midgard was located the infernal kingdom of the goddess Hel and, beyond the lands where men lived, stretched Jötunheim, the land of giants, enemies of the gods.

Yggdrasill, the cosmic tree

At the centre of the world rose the great tree Yggdrasill, the giant ash whose branches and foliage reached up to the kingdom of the gods and whose roots passed down through Midgard to hell. It was always green because it drew its power from the fountain of Urd. At the foot of this sacred tree, at the well of Urd, gushed forth the marvellous spring of the god Mímir, guaranteeing eternal wisdom. Odin had accepted sacrificing one of his eyes to drink this water so precious. On another occasion, he hung himself from the tree in order to master the runes. The gods assembled in this magic place, guarded by the Norns, goddesses destined to decide the fate of

men. Not far from there lived the dragon Nidhögg, whose principle occupation consisted of gnawing one of the roots of Yggdrasill. The tree also received milky dew from the heavens, which ran down the length of the leaves providing mead, a drink which the warriors of Odin were very fond of. A squirrel, Ratatosk, continuously ran up and down the tree trunk to sow ill feeling between the dragon, Nidhögg, and the eagle perched at the top. A stag and a goat, dispenser of the mead, also lived under the foliage of the cosmic tree. The text of the Edda (Völuspa) is very explicit:

I know that an ash-tree stands called Yggdrasill,
a high tree, soaked with shining loam;
from there come the dews which fall in the valley,
ever green, it stands over the well of fate.

From there come three girls, knowing a great deal,
from the lake which stands under tree;
Fated one is called, Becoming another –
they carved on wooden slips – Must-be the third;
they set down laws, they chose lives,
for the sons of men the fates of men.

(translation from *The Poetic Edda –*
A New Translation by Carolyne Larrington)

The cosmic tree represented the axis of universal life and protected the different worlds of Germanic mythology: Hel, the kingdom of the dead without courage; Niflheim, the land of ice; Nidavellir, the land of the dwarves; Jötunheim, the territory of the giants where the fortress Útgard stood; Midgard, the land of men; Muspelsheim, the land of fire; Svartálfaheim, the land of the dark elves; Álfheim, the land of the light elves; Vanaheim, the land of the Vanir gods; Ásgard, the citadel of the Æsir. This cosmology can, however, vary from one tradition to another. Thus the dragon Nidhögg, can also, according to certain Edda, "descend mountains of fog". The fundamental role played by Yggdrasill in Nordic mythology shows the importance attached to the tree and the forest in Germanic countries. Tacitus on several occasions describes "the divine woods" where singular rites are exercised, paying homage to the nourishing earth. Irminsûl, the trunk of the sacred ash, associated with images of the eagle, served as an idol for the Saxons. Several of these symbols were destroyed by Charlemagne in his struggle against pagan traditions during the expedition which he led in Lower Saxony

The Æsir and the Vanir

In Germanic mythology, there are two races of gods, the Æsir and the Vanir. They were at war with each other for a long time but after many changes of fortune, decided to stop fighting, preferring to live in harmony. Hostilities started when the Æsir mistreated the goddess Freyja and the witch Gullveig ("gold-draught"), from whom they wished to extract secrets. Under the guise of retaliation, the Vanir started a terrible assault on the Æsir. Contrary to all expectations, the Æsir, who counted among their ranks warrior gods without compare, had to concede defeat. The *Edda* tells the story of the campaign in several verses.

Odin shot a spear, hurled it over the host;
that was still the first war in the world;
the defensive wall was broken of the Æsir's stronghold;
the Vanir, indomitable, were trampling the plain.
(translation from *The Poetic Edda –*
A New Translation by Carolyne Larrington)

The Vanir were magnanimous and rather than destroying their valiant adversaries, chose the path of compromise. The two parties signed a peace treaty with a view to sealing their reconciliation. This lasted right up to the final episode when, in an ultimate battle (the Ragnarök), the gods united to fight against the giants.

The Æsirs, who excelled in the domains of war and magic, were, above all, soothsayers and warriors. The Vanir possessed riches, fertility and productive power. Georges Dumézil stresses in his works that this separation of attributes among the gods in fact corresponds to the three social levels inherent in Indo-European civilisation: the priests, the warriors and the farmers. A balance was established between the two higher castes and the social group of farmers and from this opposition was born the course of history.

If the war between the superior classes, represented by the Æsir, and the subordinates but holders of the economic power, represented by the Vanir, was inevitable, the reconciliation of the combatants was also inescapable. Another tradition presents the Æsirs as the gods of heaven and the Vanir as the gods of the earth. There was also a third race of gods – the Alfs – but these were less important.

The Æsir gods were more numerous; among them were Odin, Thor, Tyr, Baldr, Loki, Heimdall, Bragi, Ull while the Vanir, one of their symbols being the golden boar who moved just as easily through the heavens as under the earth, were called Njörd, Frey and Freyja. The Æsir lived in the palace of Ásgard and the Vanir in Vanaheim but this was not unchangeable. Following the great conflict that set them against each other, all the gods gathered in the kingdom of the heavens.

The Germanic gods

The Germanic myths retrace the perpetual confrontation between the gods and the giants. The gods, creators of men, established order, law and "counted time", while the giants caused chaos as they wished. It was never a question of depicting a divine, peaceful or stable society but of relating an unceasing maelstrom, a continual upheaval that could at any time lead to a Twilight of the Gods (*Götterdämmerung*), the Ragnarök of the *Edda*.

This mythology seems suitable for this warrior people, at times driven by fratricidal struggles, accustomed to the rigours of a harsh climate and always looking for new territories. Goths, Franks and Saxons called on the gods to guarantee victory in combat and to assure fertility. At the same time, they conjured up the old fears and aspired to reach Walhalla, palace of dead heroes, where they could continue to feast as they pleased. The Vikings, between the 8th and 9th century, perpetuated these traditions. Germanic mythology is presented as a tragic quest in perpetual development; against the immortality of the gods it opposes a dramatic universe where nothing is ever achieved.

Odin

Odin, the father of all, is presented as the supreme god par excellence. He is also the Wotan of the Germanic peoples of the south or the Woden of the Angles and Saxons. The Romans identified him with Mercury. In English, this is undoubtedly the origin of the word Wednesday, dedicated to Mercury. He can also be compared with Teutates, god of the Gallic tribes.

The chief of the gods, surrounded by his ravens, Hugin and Munin, Odin sat on the throne, at the foot of which waited his faithful wolves. For a warhorse, he had the spirited Sleipnir, who was unbeatable in a race, perhaps because he had eight legs.

During tempests, Odin could be seen at the head of his troops, crossing the sky in a violent rage and leading the "infernal hunt". Georges Dumézil in Mitra-Varuna stresses the violence of the symbolism: "Odhinn is the possessor of the ôdhr ('possessed' in old Scandinavian), of this Wut (fury in German). Acting at night, according also to continental beliefs, he spurred on riders of the ghostly army (das wütende Heer) of which Wode, Wodan was sometimes the head." His loyal warriors, the berserks, clothed in bear skins, assured his supremacy with their furious thirst for victory. God of war and of combat, Odin-Wotan is depicted as a soldier wearing a big cloak and riding a black horse, but he could also transform into a handsome young man or into a powerful warlord with a golden helmet and a sparkling breastplate. He possessed a magic spear, Gungnir, forged by the dwarves in the subterranean world, which never missed its target. Odin could also survey the progress of the attacks from his palace Ásgard, where he resided when he was not in Walhalla, refuge of the courageous dead. It was in this grandiose place, accompanied by the Valkyries, that he welcomed heroes fallen on the field of battle. Odin, sometimes called "Warrior Wolf", perhaps transformed into a fearsome carnivore, as did his beserks, heralding the legendary figure of the werewolf.

Odin-Wotan, god of magic, divination and wisdom, deciphered the secret of the runes. The mythological poetry of the *Words of the High One (Havama)* tells us how the supreme god achieved this. To succeed in his aim, he did not hesitate to hang himself from the cosmic tree Yggdrasill for nine days and nine nights. He also sacrificed one of his eyes to obtain the right to drink the water of the marvellous spring of Mímir. Thanks to the magic gifts which he acquired, he was also able to transform into an eagle or bear or take on the appearance of a terrible dragon. Odin, patron of the soothsayers and poets, also discovered the secret of mead: the sacred drink par excellence and source of inspiration. His two ravens, Hugin ("spirit") and Munin ("memory"), provided him with information from the most distant lands, helping him to govern his kingdom. His famous ring of gold, Draupnir, synonym for abundance, symbolised the power of the High One. Overcome with sadness, Odin threw his ring onto the funeral pyre of his son Baldr but the ring remained intact and came back to the god when Hermód returned it to him, following his journey to hell (Hel).

Odin was married to Frigg, goddess of fertility, who should not be confused with Freyja, the Vanir goddess. The chief of the gods had several conquests, notably when he courted Rind, the daughter of King Billing, or when he seduced Gunnlöd, the daughter of the giant Suttung; it was all in a good cause, however, for Odin was able to seize the secret of making mead. His wife did, however, have her revenge. Although she was unfaithful on several occasions, in particular when she had relations with Vili and Vé, the brothers of Odin, Frigg was, nevertheless, an amorous companion and attentive mother. This is demonstrated beyond doubt by her relationship with her son Baldr. Besides Baldr, Odin had several other sons: Thor, Vídar, Vali, Höd and Hermód.

Being omnipresent, Odin was not content to reign over the Empire of the Dead and participate in divine battles; he was also interested in the life of men and earthly affairs. He gave his support to the race of Völsung, who were probably his descendents. The great deeds of this line, to which Sigmund and Sigurd the dragon killers belonged, fed the legendary German tradition of the epic of the Nibelungs, which inspired Richard Wagner's Tetralogy *Der Ring des Niebelungen.*

Thor

Thor, "The Thunderer", is the god of thunder and storm. The Romans assimilated him to Jupiter and he can be compared to Taranis of the Celts or Sucellos of the Gauls. He was called Donar by the Germanic peoples of the south (Thunor in Anglo-Saxon). This is the origin of the words *Donnerstag* in German or Thursday in English, the day consecrated to Jupiter by the Romans. Very popular among the Vikings, Thor was a veritable athlete with the stature of a colossus. He stood a towering height with a great red beard and an insatiable appetite. His sparkling eyes spat lightning when he was angry. He was god of the community and protected those who cultivated the land, which explains his surname "Son of Earth" which occurs often in the *Edda*.

He crossed the sky in a chariot pulled by horses and forded rivers with great strides. A fearsome warrior, the task of fighting the giants often fell to him. He did this with power and conscience but not a great amount of genius, hence his surnames "Slaughterer", "Brother Slayer" or "First Pourer of Blood". To defeat his enemies, he used a hatchet and a hammer of stone with a

A Valkyrie
In the image of the Valkyries, "those who chose the dead" on the fields of battle, this Germania, on her proud warhorse, prepares to defend the earth of her ancestors.

short handle–Mjöllnir–which he used notably to break rocks … and the skulls of his adversaries.

Thor wore gloves of iron which enabled him to hold the burning handle of his hammer. He also had a magic belt which increased his power tenfold. Thor often cut a wretched figure next to Odin, who was much more subtle than he was. One text of the *Edda (le Lai de Barbe Grise)* puts them together in a heated dialogue and Thor is not up to the confrontation. There are, however, many legends that illustrate his deeds of valour.

One day, Thor nearly caught the great serpent of the world whose coil was threatening Midgard and provoking terrible storms. He went to find Hymir and invited him to go sea fishing. He took the precaution of changing his appearance so as not to arouse the giant's suspicion. Thor chose the most imposing of the oxen of Hymir and cut off its head. He used this as bait to lure the serpent and tossed his line into the sea. He did not have long to wait before the monster took the bait. A terrible struggle ensued and Thor nearly succeeded in landing the serpent but the giant was frightened and cut the line, allowing the monster to escape.

On another occasion, the giant, Thrym, stole Thor's hammer and as the price for returning it demanded the hand of the beautiful goddess Freyja. Before making an indignant refusal, the wise Heimdall suggested that Thor disguise himself as a woman and take on the appearance of Freyja. The subterfuge worked marvellously, despite Thor's lack of femininity and his voracity during the wedding breakfast. The crafty Loki, who was accompanying Thor, managed to allay Thrym's suspicions by explaining that the "young lady" had fasted for several days because she was very excited about the prospect of the union. The hammer was brought and placed on the knees of the bride by way of homage. Removing his veil, Thor seized his weapon and felled all the wedding guests. This comical adventure finished with the triumphant return of Thor and Loki to Ásgard. During a voyage to the kingdom of the giants, Thor fell asleep in a hut which seemed very uncomfortable. Upon waking, he was surprised to find that the aforesaid hut was, in fact, the glove of the giant Skymir. He threatened Thor, who struck him hard on the head with his hammer, only to be surprised by the reaction of the giant, who acted as if a twig had fallen on his head. Thor struck again harder but the giant contented himself with haughtily tossing his head. So "*The Thunderer*" continued along his path and arrived at the castle of continued along his path and arrived at the castle

of another giant, who gave him a series of tasks to perform: to drink a horn of beer that seemed inexhaustible, to fight against an old woman with extraordinary strength and to pick up a cat from the ground.

Thor did not manage to complete any of the tasks. As he was leaving the castle, the giant, shaken by Thor's power, finally admitted that he had been the victim of a trick. The horn of beer had been filled by the ocean; the old woman was none other than the goddess of ageing, invincible by nature; and the cat was, in fact, the great serpent of the world. Finally, the master of castle admitted that he was, in fact, Skymir and that he had fooled him! At this very moment, the scene became blurred and Skymir and his castle disappeared, as if by magic. The whole episode had been nothing but an illusion!

Once Thor/Donar also suffered losses in his battle against the giants and was injured. A Skaldic story from the 9th century describes Thor's fight against the giant Hrungnir. "*The Brawler*" was victorious but a shard from the sharpened stone of the giant became embedded in his head. A magician had to intervene and use all his talent to remove the shard of stone from the head of the child of Odin.

Thor also revealed the more pacifist aspects of his personality. His union with the goddess Sif, with hair blond like wheat, symbolised the fusion of the rainy sky and the ground which, when fertilised, produced the harvest.

Tyr

According to certain authors, Tyr would have been the principal god of the Germanic peoples but was supplanted by Odin-Wotan and Thor-Donar. He was called Tiuz by the northern peoples, Ziu by those in the south and Tiw by the Anglo-Saxons, the origin of the English word Tuesday. His characteristics, however, remain quite imprecise and rather mysterious. God of war, he was also the guarantor of pacts, conventions and treaties. This was by no means contradictory as the Germanic peoples considered that war had very precise rules. Tyr directed the *Thing*, the assembly where disputes were settled.

Even if he was more behind the scenes, Tyr remained reputed for his courage. The legend of the wolf Fenrir demonstrates his tenacity and loyalty. An oracle warned the gods: Fenrir represented a major danger and had to be rendered harmless.

Scene from the Twilight of the Gods

In the country of the gods, a Valkyrie welcomes a valiant warrior fallen in combat and gives him the cup of sacred mead.

Sandstone plaque, Mettlach 1898.

Following pages
Castle in ruins

"The castle shell appeared to me to be so dilapidated and a figure so formidable and so savage, that I swear that I would not have been surprised to see issue from below the curtains of ivy, some supernatural form wearing bizarre flowers in its apron, Gela, the betrothed of Barbarossa, or Hildegarde the wife of Charlemagne (...) I looked for a moment towards the high northern wall, with some kind of vague desire to see the goblins, that are everywhere in the north, rise brusquely from between the stones."

(The Rhine, 1842)

Victor Hugo, Indian ink, 1857

Son of the god Loki and the giantess of the ice Angrboda, Fenrir was captured and transported to Ásgard. No chain being solid enough to shackle the "Devourer", Odin asked the dwarves to make him a magic lead capable of restraining the prisoner. They performed their task diligently and, with a lot of care, manufactured a lead made of the most unlikely materials: bear tendons, the meowing of a cat, the puff of a fish, the roots of a mountain, the spittle of birds etc.

Although it had the appearance of silk, it was indestructible. If Fenrir succeeded in escaping, he would prove himself all powerful. The terrible wolf accepted being chained but he was suspicious and demanded that one of the gods put his hand in his mouth during the test. Without hesitation, Tyr held his hand between the jaws of the monster. The lead was passed around Fenrir's neck. Despite all of his efforts, he could not manage to break the magic chain but, as an act of revenge, he bit off poor Tyr's hand with his powerful teeth. Having lost an arm, the god of war lost his pride and was relegated to a background role. This episode can be compared to the misadventure of the Celtic god Nuada, who lost his hand during the first battle of Mag Tured. Mutilated by fidelity to the community of gods, Tyr would later have to confront another monstrous wolf during Ragnarök.

He can also be compared to Forsete or Forsita, god of justice that the Friesians called Forsite.

Baldr

The legendary figure of Baldr, also called Balder or Baldur, appears very original in the pantheon of Germanic gods. The son of Odin and Frigg, Baldr was as a beautiful young man, who spread happiness all around him. From a very young age, however, he was afflicted by terrible nightmares that haunted his nights, predicting his imminent demise. Peace-loving and benevolent, Baldr embodies the positive elements of Germanic mythology.

He was pursued, perhaps by an ancient curse, or by the demon of jealousy exercising its ravages. In order to cast out the evil spell, Frigg set off on a long voyage to different worlds, visiting the kingdom of the dead, the land of giants, not forgetting Midgard, and made each being and each thing promise never to act detrimentally to the life of her son. In her quest,

Frigg seemed to have forgotten nothing, neither water nor fire nor the monsters nor the fiercest animals. She had also thought of illnesses, the slight and the serious and the imponderable. The gods wanted to test the invulnerability of Baldr, and decided to gather together. Things looked promising but they had not taken into account the perfidy of Loki. He had learned that Frigg in her noble endeavour had committed a major error: She had forgotten to ask the mistletoe not to harm her son. The little plant had seemed too puny to her and she had not bothered to ask it to take an oath.

Loki lost no time in cutting a branch of mistletoe and made his way to the gathering of the gods – the *Thing* – where the test had already commenced. Everyone was forcefully throwing stones, spears, daggers, hatchets and burning stakes at Baldr but nothing was able to injure him. Loki approached Baldr's brother, Höd, the blind god, and placed the branch of mistletoe in his hand, exhorting him to take part in the game. Skilfully guided by Loki, Höd violently hurled the branch in the direction of his brother, who was pierced and collapsed, mortally wounded.

A grandiose funeral was organised in memory of the happy Baldr, whose remains were burnt on a pyre before being placed on his *drakkar* (boat) The boat was also set alight and pushed towards the open sea. It soon disappeared from view and was enveloped in the gloom. Frigg was inconsolable and managed to convince Hermód to make his way to the kingdom of Hel to bring back Baldr. Since he had not died in battle, he was disgraced and not in Walhalla.

Hermód started out on his mission straight away. He borrowed the valiant Sleipnir from his father Odin and, after nine days, reached the gates of hell. He offered a ransom for Baldr but Hel replied that she would only let the noble god leave on the condition that all the beings of the universe wept for him and prayed for his resurrection. Again, the gods set about the task and came very close to success: even the stones were sad … but Thökk, a giantess of the ice, was insensitive and refused to have anything to do with the general mourning: "Hel should keep that which she possesses!" So Baldr could not leave Hel. The wrath of the gods increased when they realised that Thökk was none other than Loki, who had changed his appearance to accomplish his misdemeanour.

The disappearance of Baldr had serious repercussions and heralded the imminent arrival of Ragnarök. So the ancient world collapsed and the most beautiful of the Æsirs were able to return to govern the new order of a world purified by the catastrophe.

Loki

Loki, the son of a giant, was the god of fire and husband of the giantess Angrboda. He also had three extraordinary children: the wolf Fenrir, the great serpent of the world and Hel, the goddess of Hell.

This singular character occupies a special place in Germanic mythology. Half god, half demon, he did not feel solidarity with the beings among whom he lived. Although he stayed most often in the castle of Ásgard and was part of the clan of Æsirs, Loki could not help but to spread discord and to behave like a malicious creature. He also adopted an ambiguous attitude towards Thor and made fun of his oafishness. Baldr's death and his banishment to hell were due to the wickedness of Loki.

One day, a giant proposed to the gods to erect a huge rampart around Ásgard. In exchange he demanded the hand of Freyja, the goddess of love. The gods accepted the measure, convinced that the giant would not manage to finish the work in the time agreed. Loki intervened and gave the giant a magic horse which enabled him to do an amazing amount of work, and move blocks of stones weighing several tonnes in a few instants. The gods were annoyed at Loki's behaviour and ordered him to take charge of the situation. He took the form of a mare who managed to lead the magic horse far away.

On another occasion, for no apparent reason, he cut the blond hair of the goddess Sif, the wife of Thor. When Thor caught sight of this, he wanted to strangle Loki but with his customary skill, the demonic creature managed to appease him. To redeem himself, he asked the dwarves to make golden hair for the beautiful Sif.

Loki even delivered the goddess Idun, holder of the apples of eternal youth, to the giant Thjazi. Deprived of the presence of the magic fruit, the gods started to age and Odin, gathering his forces, implored Loki to retrieve Idun. After changing into a falcon, he reached Jötunheim. By a ruse, he managed to seize the goddess, whom he changed into a nut in order to more easily take her to Ásgard. The giant Thjazi, who had taken the appearance of an eagle, tried to follow them but was finally burnt by the fire that the gods had set at the summit of the citadel. The gods always indulged Loki despite his escapades and treachery. The episode of the banquet of Ægir was to precipitate events. Ægir, one of the most ancient Germanic gods, sometimes also considered a giant, reigned over the ocean. He periodically abandoned the depths of the sea to organise grand celebrations to which he invited all the gods. Loki decided to invite himself to the banquet; always the unwelcome guest, the atmosphere became icy when he entered the grand hall where the assembly was being held.

In the name of the laws of hospitality, Odin imposed the presence of Loki on everyone. Far from being grateful, he proceeded to verbally attack the gods. Insulting several of the guests, he concentrated his attentions particularly on the goddesses Idun, Frigg and Gefjon, recalling their moral turpitude with formidable precision. He even revealed the good fortune which he had had with some of them, in particular the beautiful Sif, wife of Thor. Up to that point, the latter had not been present at the banquet because he was on a mission to the far lands of the east but, at that moment, he burst into the middle of the guests. With a great to-do, "The Thunder" threatened Loki with his glowing hammer and the troublemaker decided to beat his retreat. As he left the assembly, Loki uttered terrible threats to those present.

Loki had gone too far and the gods decided to put an end to his machinations. They set out in pursuit of him and, to escape them, he changed into a salmon. Thanks to his piercing eyes, Heimdall located the fish, which was caught in Odin's nets. Loki was taken to a cave and solidly attached to a large rock, close to which was hiding an enormous serpent. Burning venom escaped from the mouth of the serpent and ran down Loki's face. His second wife, Sigyn, collected the venom in a cup but each time she had to empty it, the venom continued to ooze and the burns started again. The suffering was such that the unfortunate wretch writhed with pain, making the earth tremble. If Loki suffered this terrible torture to the end, it was because he knew that he would soon escape. He was waiting for Ragnarök and preparing to lead the forces of evil lined up against the gods.

Following pages
The round of stars

"My daughters are waiting for you impatiently.

It is they who bring the night round.

They indulge you in their dances and their songs.

My father, my father, do you not see over there,

Dancing in the shadows, the daughter of the Alder King?"

Goethe, Alder King (1786)

Composition of Hermann Hendrich about 1900.

Heimdall

This was the guardian of the Germanic gods. He controlled and monitored access to the kingdom of the sky. Heimdall stayed on the bridge of Bilfröst, ready to sound the alarm at the slightest hint of danger. It is from here that he blew his trumpet, Gjall, on the day of the Twilight of the Gods. The god of light, Heimdall is also named "Sparkle of the world" (*Edda*). Blessed with exceptional vision, he could see the slightest movement of troops for more than a hundred and fifty kilometres (93 miles)around. Thanks to his sharp hearing, he could hear leaves fall when the giant of the forests (the wind) appeared.

Under the name of Ríg, Heimdall visited the earth and contributed to the creation of three classes of men: the serf (thræl), destined for hard labour on the land; the peasant (karl), freeman; and the nobleman (jarl), accustomed to handling arms and an expert in the art of war.

Heimdall was also the sworn enemy of Loki. One day, the latter stole the magnificent necklace of Freyja and hid it on a lost island. Heimdall had seen everything from his vantage point and set off in pursuit of his adversary. Taking the form of a seal, he succeeded in reaching the small island and attacked Loki. Following a duel, Heimdall managed to floor his old enemy, retrieving the jewel and returning it to the goddess. This merciless struggle between the forces of light and darkness was set to conclude during Ragnarök, when Heimdall and Loki would have their final confrontation.

The Vanir gods

The Vanir were more pacifist in nature and radiated kindness and bliss. Deities of fertility, richness and health, they lived in Vanaheim but often visited Ásgard, the home of the Æsir. After the war between the gods and the agreement that followed, Njörd, Frey and Freyja lived in the citadel of Ásgard. Njörd was the Germanic god of the seas and navigators. He was benevolent by nature and often calmed tempests started by the dark Ægir and his wife Rán. Appreciated by sailors and fishermen, "the great blower" (he created favourable winds) came to the aid of lost ships. Surrounded by seagulls and seals, Njörd liked to rest in a quiet bay under cover of the swell. He married his own sister Nerthus, described by Tacitus, but when he reached Ásgard, they had to separate, as the Æsirs condemned sexual relations between brother and sister.

He then married Skadi, the daughter of a giant, but it was an unhappy union. Njörd found it very difficult living in Jötunheim, the land of ice and fog where Skadi resided and his wife did not appreciate the crashing of waves and crying of seagulls. She preferred the howling of wolves and long walks in cold lands to sea breezes.

Frey was the son of Njörd. God of the sun, fertility and prosperity, he also reigned over the country of Álfheim, the home of the light elves. He possessed a magic sword, one of the rays of the sun which fought on its own, and a *drakkar* (boat), Skídbladnir, which always steered itself in whatever direction Frey desired. A symbolic representation of the clouds, his vessel travelled on the sea, the earth and through the air. It could transport an entire army but could also be slipped into a pocket, as if it had been folded. Frey also travelled through the skies in a chariot made of gold, pulled by a boar, the symbol of the Vanir. Frey fell head over heels in love with Gerd (Gerdr), the daughter of the giant Gymir. His servant, Skírnir, triumphantly brought him the beautiful goddess. He had to employ his powers of ingenuity because Gerd proved very stubborn and refused all the presents offered by Skírnir: the ring of Odin, eleven apples of gold and many other gifts besides. She finally relented when Skírnir threatened to engrave maleficent runes under her name,which would compel her to live alone "forgotten by everyone". Accepting that she must follow the servant of Frey, Gerd promised to meet her betrothed nine days later in a sacred forest. It is said that she felt her heart of ice melt when she finally met her intended.

Freyja, daughter of Njörd and sister of Frey is often confused with Frigg (Frija), goddess of fertility and wife of Odin-Wotan. Also a goddess of fertility, Freyja was, however, more aggressive as she accompanied the gods on the field of battle and led the Valkyries. Paul Hermann, in his *German Mythology*, identifies her with Fricke of the popular legends of Pomerania and with Mother Holle, celebrated all over Germany. She is sometimes represented on a chariot pulled by cats. Freyja was an expert in magic and cried tears of gold. She also adored jewellery and never hesitated to pay with her person to satisfy her passion. She coveted a marvellous solid gold necklace kept by the dwarves and, in order to obtain it, had to spend the night with the four dwarves that had crafted it.

Being extremely beautiful, Freyja had many adventures and legions of pretenders. The giant Thrym,

thief of the hammer of Thor, wished to marry her, as did the giant who built the walls of Ásgard. She also took a human called Ottar as a lover. She changed him into a boar to keep him with her, and rode him across the domain of the skies. Goddess of love and of pleasure, Freyja evoked the figure of Venus. It is for this reason that Friday, the day devoted to Venus by the Romans, was chosen by the Anglo-Saxons and by the Germans (*Freitag*) to honour her memory.

The secondary deities

Many other gods populated the Germanic pantheon. We have already mentioned some of them, such as Bragi, the god of poetry, husband of the seductive Idun, who kept the magic apples of eternal youth. During the famous banquet of Ægir, he was the first to reproach Loki for coming to cause trouble at the celebration. In the 9th century, there lived in Norway a celebrated skald called Bragi Boddason, known as Bragi the Old. In his stories, he tells of the deeds of Thor, Odin, the Valkyrie, Hild, and of Gefjon and Hel. It is very possible that, after his death, Bragi the Old was accorded the status of a god and confused with the patron of the skalds, Bragi: It is even more likely that he appeared later as a god in Germanic mythology.

Hœnir, on the other hand, seems to be a much more ancient god. One of the Edda has him taking part in an adventure at the side of Odin and Loki. He was the brother of Odin, who sent him to the court of the Vanir as a token of goodwill at the start of the conflict between the two races of gods. Hœnir, however, disappointed the Vanir with his continual hesitation and his inability to make a decision. He always referred to his companion, the wise Mímir, before taking a decision. The exasperated Vanir, having the opportunity to demonstrate their savagery, ended up by decapitating Mímir and sending his head to the Æsir. Odin intervened to return life to the precious head by rubbing it with magic herbs. He then placed it under the tree, Yggdrasill, to guard the magic well of Urd.

Vídar, a solitary and silent god, is one of the sons of Odin. His principal claim to glory was surviving the cataclysm of Ragnarök, during which he managed to kill the wolf Fenrir, avenging his father. Váli, the son of Odin and Rind, also escaped destruction during the Twilight of the Gods. He had killed his half brother, Höd, beforehand. Ull, a rather mysterious crea-

ture, often passed as the god of winter. A great athlete and accomplished hunter, he crossed expanses of ice looking for game. Reputed for his wisdom, he sometimes played the role of an arbitrator. According to certain legends, Ull even replaced Odin at the head of the gods for a time, when the latter, accused of devoting too much attention to feminine conquests, was banished.

Hel, goddess of hell and the kingdom of the dead, was not by any means an evil goddess, even though her father was Loki. She did, nevertheless, have one surprising peculiarity: one side of her face was white and the other black. She lived in a subterranean kingdom, either the kingdom of icy fog, Niflheim, or the territory that bore her name, Hel. Her residence never appeared terrifying and it is a long way from the hell of Christianity. The dead that resided there led a peaceful existence, not to be compared with the feverish activity that reigned in Walhalla.

Volund occupies a special place in the universe of secondary gods, since it is he that forged the weapons of the warriors. In his underground workshop, he also crafted jewellery and golden ornaments. Son of a mermaid, he may have had something in common with the world of the dwarves because of his activities as a craftsman. The Germanic peoples of the south called him Welund and the Anglo-Saxons Wayland.

Spirits, Demons and Sorcerers

Besides the most varied gods and deities, Germanic mythology also presents a considerable range of supernatural creatures, each as surprising as the next: Kindly spirits of nature, evil spirits, Valkyries, Norns, fairies, witches, genies, dwarves, elves, giants etc. In his work devoted to *The Rhine* (1842), Victor Hugo paints a striking picture of this universe:

"When the dawn of the rebirth of civilisation started to appear on the Taunus, there was, on the banks of the Rhine, an adorable murmuring of legends and fables; in all parts illuminated by this distant ray, there were a thousand supernatural and charming characters resplendent all at once, whereas, in the dark parts, lurked hideous forms and frightening phantoms.

A daughter of the water

Genies of the forest and legends from Germany: An abundant universe where the myths of the infernal hunt, Diane and the daughters of water mix...
Engraving from about 1900

Following pages
Legends and sorcery
The Devil celebrates the joyous dance of the witches on the Brocken in Saxony.

am 1. Mai

While were being built with beautiful new basalt, next to Roman ruins, today no longer there, the Saxon and Gothic castles, today completely destroyed, an entire population of imaginary beings, in direct communication with beautiful women and handsome knights, spreads throughout the Rhingau.

The nymphs who lived in the wood, the water sprites who lived in the water, the gnomes who lived inside the earth, the spirit of the rocks, the striker, the black hunter crossing the thicket, mounted on a great stag with sixteen antlers; the virgin of the black swamp; the six virgins of the red marsh; Wodan; the god with ten hands; the twelve black men; (...) Everard the Barbarian, who advised the princes lost in the hunt; Siegfried the horned one, who felled dragons in their caves."

Spirits and errant souls

Like the Celts, the Germanic peoples attached great importance to nature and the elements. Many myths feature benevolent or harmful spirits who lived in rivers, lakes, springs, waterfalls, mountains and forests. The colours of the rivers reflected the humour of the spirits who lived in them, while the "giant of the forests" was able to blow more or less strongly according to his will. According to circumstances, these spirits could help men to have great fish catches or to track game in far lands. A stock breeder, whose stock had been decimated by battle, was visited by a spirit of the earth who came to him in a dream. The next morning, two goats, which seemed to come from nowhere, joined his herd which, as if by an enchantment, became prosperous again.

Theoprastus Bombastus von Hohenheim, known as Paracelsus, listed the "elementary spirits", nymphs and water sprites in the water; sylphs in the air; gnomes in the earth; salamanders in the fire. Salamandre, whom Victor Hugo met in his voyage along the Rhine: "It was the mysterious and solitary inhabitant of this ruin, the beast spirit, the animal both real and fabulous..."

The Germanic peoples thought that during sleep, the spirit of the man detached from his body and travelled in space, like a "double" or a "guardian angel". This is the *Doppelgänger* of popular German traditions. The soul could be understood as a breath, a shadow or a fog. Nowadays, the tradition of blowing out the candles on a birthday cake is linked to these ancient beliefs. This is probably why one should never celebrate a birthday in advance, because candles should only be blown out for years that have already passed, otherwise the person involved risks dying during that year. The Scandinavians called this shadow *fylgia*, an expression which one cannot help comparing to the *fjelde* of Norway: immense plateaux, deserted and sinister dominated peaks worn by glacial erosion. The fantastic rock formations and steep mountains evoked, for many of the inhabitants, cohorts of giants. Are the Picts of Iceland not called *jokul*, which comes from *jotun* (giant)!

Pitted against the wild elements, represented by some sea monster or evil giant, there were always good genies, ready to re-establish the balance in order to defend the ship in distress or the threatened crop. These same spirits could also rise up against those who dared to invade the earth of the ancestors, and lend a helping hand to the warlords.

Vast German forests in Thuringia, Bohemia or East Prussia; the Baltic coast of Denmark; the fjords of Norway; the bubbling springs of Iceland; the immense lakes in Sweden... In these wooded countries with vast frozen areas, it is easy to imagine the emotional force of the myths and legends. The giants of the ice, the tempest or the fog crossed snow-covered slopes or the desolate islands of the North Sea and the Baltic, personifying all powerful nature. This sentiment of insecurity was always reinforced by the fact that the northern part of Scandinavia had six months of day and six months of night.

The Valkyries and Walhalla

Surrounded by great prestige, the Valkyries were the virgin warriors who escorted Odin and surveyed the fields of battle, riding proudly upon their wild stallions. They also selected the dead warriors in combat (*einherjar*) and accompanied them to Walhalla. Those "Who Chose the Dead" were originally deadly spirits, drinkers of blood, who tore open cadavers like birds of prey.

They are represented as the companions of ravens, who descended on the remains of soldiers to tear them to shreds. Fearsome warriors, they evoke the Amazons of Antiquity. A skaldic text from the 6th century reveals the song of the Valkyries:

"We tear, we tear
The material from the spear
Where the standard goes through
Of the male warriors;
Not letting his life escape;
Selectors of the dead;
We choose those who die."]
(Renauld-Krantz, Anthologie de la poésie
nordique ancienne)

Once a warrior saw the tragic Valkyrie appear suddenly at his side, he knew that death was imminent. The "Bearers of Shields" then appeared on a less sombre day and became the attentive companions of the High One. The Romantic imagery presents us with a picture of beautiful princesses with long blond hair and generous figures, wearing armour and a winged helmet. The Valkyries welcomed the warriors to Walhalla, where they provided them with the best of care. They served them large portions of meat and poured them lots of heavenly mead in cups or sacred horns.

It sometimes came to pass that these superb creatures fell in love with the gods or even simple mortals, particularly when they came to bathe in the lakes and the rivers. Some of them assumed the appearance of graceful female swans. One legend tells of how the blacksmith god, Welund, one day surprises three young girls bathing in a pond; he steals the swan plumage, which they have left on the bank, and is allowed to keep them for nine years. For allowing herself to be seduced by a mortal, the Valkyrie Brunhild is punished by Wotan, who shuts her in a vast castle surrounded by flames. This is one of the themes of the epic of the Nibelungs. The Valkyries appear on many stones sculpted in the Viking period, notably in Sweden.

Walhalla, the marvellous palace of the dead warriors, was built to house the army of heroes who would fight on the side of the gods in the final combat. Its roof was constructed of gleaming shields, shining with a thousand flames. This gigantic temple had more than five hundred doors which were each large enough to allow rows of almost five hundred men to pass at the same time. While waiting for the Twilight of the Gods, the warriors, reduced to the state of phantoms, led, nevertheless, a pleasant existence and practiced the handling of weapons.

Odin lived in Walhalla, surrounded by soldiers who lived a joyous life, partaking of many feasts, where they were served the meat of wild boar. Mead, beer and magic milk flowed in abundance. A magic cauldron cooked delicious boar stew which never ran out. Knowing that they would have to fight the giants in a terrible battle, the gods were relying greatly on the warriors of Walhalla to provide the ultimate contingents of fighters, who would fight right to the end of the unleashing of the forces of evil. In the Wagnerian version of the myth, which is described in *The Rhine Gold* (1868) or in *Siegfried* (1876), the first Valkyries are the daughters of Wotan and Erda, personification of the spirit of the earth.

Between 1830 and 1842, not far from Regensburg in Bavaria, King Louis I had the temple of Walhalla constructed in honour of the Germanic armies. The monument that, from some distance, is reminiscent of the Parthenon, is set apart at the dark end of beautiful forest. Louis I of Bavaria also had a temple of deliverance (*Befreiungshalle*) constructed, near Kelheim upstream from Regensburg, to celebrate Germanity and the memory of the battle of nations, a terrible conflict which took place in Leipzig in October 1813.

Norns, fairies, witches and phantasmagoria

In the image of the Fates, spinners of Antiquity, the Norns, goddesses of destiny and of passing time, decided the destiny of men but also that of the gods. Three in number, they remained around the well of Urd, under the cosmic tree Yggdrasill. Their names were Urd ("destiny" or "past"), Verlandi ("present") and Skuld ("future"). According to tradition, it is Urd who warns Odin-Wotan that he will succumb to the sly attacks of the wolf Fenrir during Ragnarök.

The fairies are definitely the descendents of the Norns. Mythological feminine beings endowed with magic powers, fairies have an important place in almost all of the mythologies of the world; the nymphs of Greek Antiquity, like the Hathors of ancient Egypt, belong to the same family. Fairies are very present in Celtic imagery, with symbolic figures such as Morgan or Vivien, and they also appear in Germanic mythology – to such an extent that certain heroines foreign to the Nordic tradition sometimes amalgamated with the legends from Germany. The story of Melusina, protector of the Poitiers house of Lusignan, likewise became one of the favourite themes in German poetry from the 17th century onwards, and especially in the Romantic period.

Frederick I Barbarossa, emperor of Germany from 1152 to 1190. He died during the 3rd crusade but his aura was such among the Germanic community that a legend was born to perpetuate his memory. Henceforth, Frederick Barbarossa would sleep in the mountain of Kyffhaüser, in Thuringia, waiting for the predestined moment when he would reappear and return Germany to her eternal greatness.

Engraving of 1921 Frankenhausen.

In the 16th century, Paracelsus was interested in nymphs and water sprites. It is true that this water sprite with long blond hair and the tail of a serpent, often represented with the wings of a bat, had everything with which to seduce the Germanic peoples. The water sprites or nixies were more evil and tried to attract handsome knights, who were lost, in order to drown them or to take them off to their crystal palace at the end of the waters. The swan, the immaculate bird, is often merely the animal form taken by fairies, Valkyries or water sprites – virgins in the pool of Novalis. Sometimes the swan was the sign of evil spells. In the fairytale by Anderson, *The Traveling Companion*, a bloodthirsty virgin appears in the form of a black swan. The enchantment ceased when the swan was plunged into purifying water: The swan became white and the young woman changed into a beautiful princess.

In 1811, Friedrich de La Motte-Fouqué published *Ondine*, a story which inspired Goethe, and which Hoffmann later transformed into an opera. These daughters of the water, who haunted rivers, reflected the myth of the Lorelei, the water sprite of the Rhine. The legend was born on the banks of the great river, not far from Saint Goar, at the point where the Rhine has quite a dangerous curve, which frightened many a boatman. Their fear was amplified even more by the phenomenon of the echo, which rings in these sombre gorges. From the top of the great ragged rock that bears its name, the Lorelei (*lei* in the Rhineland dialect means "rock") called to the boatmen like a mermaid. Distracted by her beauty, they forgot to steer their rudders and their boats crashed into the rocks. Clemens Brentano, Joseph von Eichendorff, Heine and Appolinaire sang of "the beautiful Loreley", "her eyes the colours of the Rhine and her hair of the sun". Victor Hugo described the site for us: "On the savagest of bends, leading into and precipitating at a point in the Rhine, with its thousand beds of granite, lending it the appearance of a crumbling staircase, the fabulous rock of the Loreley. There, there is a famous echo, which, they say, repeats seven times all that one says or all that one sings." (*The Rhine*).

In the same way as the Norns, the magicians or the banshees of Ireland, the fairies are the messengers of the Other World. They determine destiny in the stories. These are the good fairies that lean over the cradles of the newborn and endow them with beautiful qualities, as in Sleeping Beauty. In a manuscript from the 13 century, Huon de Bordeaux, Auberon (or Oberon) also tells of his origins: "When I was born, there was great rejoicing: all the knights of the kingdom were invited and the fairies came to visit my mother. One of them must have been ill-disposed, because she gave me the gift which you behold. I became a little hunchbacked dwarf ... The second fairy was more generous: thanks to her, I know the thoughts and plans of all ... The third fairy gave me even more: to improve my lot and favour me, she gave me the following gift: regardless of the country, frontiers or kingdoms, ... where I would like to be in the name of God, the moment I ask, I will be accompanied there by as many men as I like". (*the story of Huon de Bordeaux and Oberon, King of the Fairies*)

When the fairy was evil, she came closer to sorcery. From the Middle Ages up to the 17th century, witches supposedly communicated with the Devil, who gave them supernatural power. On the Sabbath, they travelled on broomsticks to participate in satanic rituals. Each year, on the night of the Walpurgis (30 April – 1 May), witches gathered in the Brocken, at the summit of the Hartz massif in Saxony, where they held a great Sabbath, immortalised in Goethe's *Faust*. They also gathered at Hörselberg in Thuringia or on the Stauffenstein in Franconia. From the 14th and 15th centuries onwards, sorcery was suppressed throughout Europe, particularly in Germany. The *Maleus Maleficarum* or Hammer of the Witches, re-edited more than thirty times between 1487 and 1669, remains the most famous of the works on demonology, due to the frenzied minds of Jakob Sprenger and Heinrich Kramer.

To continue on this little survey of the phantasmagoria, we must speak of the singular creatures known as lycanthropes. Spirits of the wood that appeared to hunt travellers, the werewolves are most often men transformed into savage beasts. Any man bitten by a werewolf became a lycanthrope himself. Sometimes, Satan took the appearance of a wolf to preside over the ceremonies of the Sabbath. In the 11th century, a bishop of Worms declared that certain witches or wicked fairies of destiny could transform any man into a werewolf. Johann Geiler from Kaysersberg, the author of a work on sorcery, published in Germany in the 16th century, thought that only the Devil could claim such a transformation.

The daughters
of the water

"The mermaid, who sings with a voice so beautiful that she bewitches men with her singing, teaches to those who have to navigate this world, that which is necessary to improve themselves". (Guillaume de Clerc, Bestiaire divin, 13th century). [Divine Bestiary]

Water sprites, mermaids and daughters of the water appear from a cave in an attempt to attract sailors and navigators etc.

Chants sur l'eau, Jean-Francis Auburtin (1866-1930)
Musée de Petit Palais, Paris.

The legends of werewolves continued in Germany and all of central Europe for a long time. There are very few examples of female werewolves; on the other hand, the daughters of the forest are many, such as Agatha in the opera of Carl Maria von Weber, *Der Freischütz*.

Dwarves, imps and elves

As we saw during the birth of the world, the dwarves lived underground. Small and sometimes deformed, they sported beards and hats. Mostly kindly, the dwarves had to avoid coming up above ground because they would be turned to stone. Very skilled and industrious, the dwarves sometimes resembled miners working in the subterranean galleries and they also dressed similarly: leather belt and apron, lantern, axe and hammer. We hear about them a lot in the Brothers Grimm story *Snow White and the Seven Dwarves*. They prove themselves to be extraordinary blacksmiths and excellent goldsmiths. The objects (weapons, jewellery etc.), which they manufacture for the gods, are innumerable. Odin was very grateful, as they made him his ring of gold, Draupnir, and his magic spear, Gungnir. The dwarves also made Mjöllnir, the hammer of Thor; Skídbladnir, the ship of Frey; and Brísingamen, the necklace of gold coveted by Freyja. To thank them for all their marvellous work, the gods promised to give one of the dwarves, called Alvís, the hand of Thrúd, the daughter of Thor, in marriage. The latter, however, was opposed to the marriage and for once proved himself to be the shrewder. When Alvís went to find him, Thor submitted the dwarf to a series of questions before giving him his daughter. Engaged in answering the questions, Alvís did not see the time passing and, in the morning, was changed into stone by the first rays of the sun.

The dwarves stole from the wise Kvasir the secret formula for mead but they did not keep it for long, because it was stolen from them by an ice giant called Suttung. Odin, in turn, heard speak of the marvellous beverage and decided to seize it. With this aim, he set out for Jötunheim and paid court to the beautiful Gunnlöd, daughter of Suttung. She allowed him to drink the enchanted mead and, upon leaving for Ásgard in the form of an eagle, Odin took care to conserve a little of the precious drink at the back of his mouth. When he arrived, he spat the mead out into a jug.

Tireless explorers of the underground and the mines, the dwarves sometimes discovered fabulous treasure. They appropriated these treasures and became the guardians of them. The dwarf Andvari also possessed a marvellous treasure but lost it to Loki. In order to rescue Odin and Hœnir, held prisoner by Hreidmar, Loki set off in search of the treasure kept by Andvari. Arriving on the shores of a subterranean lake, he caught a large pike, which happened to be none other than the dwarf. Under threat, Loki managed to obtain his treasure, including a magnificent ring of gold, whose essential virtue was the constant provision of infinite riches. Whilst Loki was resting, Andvari cast a spell on the ring which, from that point onwards, would cause the death of the person who possessed it. The prophecy was fulfilled. Loki gave the treasure to Hreidmar, who was killed shortly afterwards by his son Fáfnir, who transformed into a dragon and was slain by Sigurd.

Epic German poetry uses the same story, slightly transposed in the *Lay of the Nibelungs*, where Siegfried fights the dwarf Alberich. In *The Rhine Gold* (1868), *Siegfried* (1876) and *Twilight of the Gods* (1876), Richard Wagner introduces Alberich. His role is of the utmost importance since, by stealing the gold from the Rhine and forging the all-powerful ring, the dwarf heralds the fateful tragedy.

Some authors claim that there are thousands of types of dwarves and we certainly know several terms used to describe them: imps, kobals, cobales, kobolds, goblins, gibelins, goguelins, farfadets, follets, gnomes, korrigan goblins, sotrès, sylvans, elves etc. They are called *Brownies* in Scotland, *Heinzelmännchen*, *Trudenmännchen* or *Wicht* in Germany, *drals* in Auvergne and *folletons* in Dauphiné.

Imps in the image of Trilby created by Charles Nodier are small, mischievous creatures, rarely evil. Cobales, like dwarves, visit mines and amass treasure. If they are not disturbed in their work, they are normally peaceful. The kobold, who wears the red bonnet, can, on the other hand, be much more disagreeable. "Honoured by the valets, servants and cooks of Germany, the kobold is very helpful … It is not advisable to neglect them, however. If a cook neglects them, she can do nothing right; she breaks the china; she knocks over or spoils the sauces; and when the master of the house scalds her, she hears the kobold burst out laughing behind her. If he has received an insult, the scene becomes more tragic; he places poison or the blood of a viper in the dishes; sometimes, he even wrings the neck of the imprudent valet who tormented him." (Abbé Migné, Dictionnaire des sciences occultes, 1848).

The goblins, friendly demons par excellence, hide in the recesses of houses. They evoke the domestic demons of Scandinavian countries who offer their services to the inhabitants. Ronsard alluded to them in one of his poems. Imps live in witches' lairs and disturb the tranquillity of the churches. The goguelins prefer to frequent the hold and the space between the decks of ships. Hobgoblins, often compared to fairies, seem to be directly under the authority of Lucifer. Assuming many different forms, they take pleasure in causing trouble for couples, frightening young women and slipping into the beds of married women. The gnomes, small, hideous creatures, hide in the depths of the earth. A tribe of gnomes lived on the Lorelei rock. The korrigan goblins cross lands and dance around menhirs. The sortès meet mostly in the forests of the Vosges. The sylvans haunt the forests, pursuing any women that venture there.

Elves (from the old German *alp* which is equivalent to our modern word "nightmare") symbolise, in Nordic countries, more the forces of nature and reside in the forests. Although the English authors of the Middle Ages revered them, the Germans feared them. Very malicious, they are sometimes wily and like dancing in the night, under the moonlight, in clearings or on desolate heaths. Woe betide he who dare interrupt these farandoles: The elves bring him into their round and turn him until he dies. Victor Hugo also speaks of this in a very evocative way:

"I seemed to hear the familiar genies of the Rhine, the dulaendes and the gnomes repeated them in my ear with mocking laughter. It was just the hour where they appeared, mixed with sylphides, masks, magicians and brucolaques, and where they go for their mysterious dances which leave large circular traces on the downtrodden grass, traces which the cows look at, dreaming, the next morning." (The Rhine).

Théophile Gautier immortalised his little maleficent deities in his famous verses:

"C'est la nuit que les elfes sortent
Avec leur robe humide au bord,
Et sur les nénuphars emportent
Leur valseur de fatigue mort."

"It is the night when the elves come out
With their robes damp at the seams
And on the waterlillies they carry
Their dance of tired death."

Oberon, close to the dwarf Alberich, was the King of the Elves. He is found in several famous works such as the epic poem *Huon de Bordeaux* (about 1260); *A Midsummer Night's Dream* (1595) by William Shakespeare; *Oberon* (1780) by Christoph Martin Wieland; or the eponymous opera of Carl Maria von Weber. In the Danish ballad upon which Goethe based his *Erlkönig* (The Alder King), the Princess of the Elves sacrifices the knight who did not wish to follow her.

The giants

They are not very different from the giants of Greek mythology, locked up by Zeus, or from the giants of Irish stories, of whom Balor remains the most representative. Although older than the gods and ruling over the forces of nature, the giants were pushed into inhospitable areas which were very cold, Jötunheim, not far from Niflheim, the lands of icy fog. They have a certain bitterness and, as we have seen, make formidable enemies for the gods. Kindly giants are rare.

Besides Ymir, the first of the giants, there was also Angrboda, ice giantess and wife of Loki; Geirröd, the ice giant who nearly triumphed over Thor; Gjálp, the daughter of Geirröd, who could transform a peaceful river into a devastating torrent; Gríd, the good giantess who helped Thor to fight Geirröd; Hrungnir, the strongest of the giants who defied Odin in a horse race and nearly managed to beat him; Hymir, the possessor of a barrel so vast that it could hold enough beer to satisfy all the gods; Surt, giant of fire, who appeared suddenly from Muspelsheim, the burning country, during Ragnarök; Thjazi, ice giant who changed into an eagle; Thrym, the ice giant who stole Thor's hammer; etc.

In almost every case, the gods defeat the giants but during a final combat, the creatures of the ice take their revenge. We notice that these creatures survive in the Germanic legends of the Middle Ages: giants of the forest, the fog, the air, the tempests or the mountains. The water giant of ancient Germanic beliefs, Mimiô probably corresponds to the Nordic Mímir, inspiration for the sacred spring.

The Twilight of the Gods

In the same way that the Greek inhabitants of Olympia fought the Titans, the Nordic gods' last battle was with the giants. The Germanic peoples did not believe in the eternity of their world any more than they believed in the invincibility of their gods; these remained subject to destiny and, since they were not infallible, would one day have to pay the price for their crimes and their errors. The war between the Æsir and the Vanir, symbol of a battered and divided universe, was the sign heralding the "destiny" of the gods, the *Götterdämmerung*. The death of Baldr, the god pure of all compromise, was definitely the trigger. One of the texts of *Edda*, *The Seeress's Prophecy* (Völuspa) describes in great detail this last episode, which would lead to the end of the world.

Three years of unending winter wore away the resistance of the gods while the giants mobilised. All around the walls of Ásgard, hate and resentment grew, prefiguring the unleashing of the forces of evil. Society rapidly started to break down. On the earth, nothing remained sacred: brother fought against brother and parents disowned their children. Iron, fire and the eternal frost would soon reign. A pack of terrible wolves, the sons of Fenrir, suddenly appeared from the lands of the east. One of them seized the sun and undertook to devour it. So it was that night spread over the domain of the gods. Cries of alarm were heard from all sides. In the camp of the Æsirs, Crête d'Or called the tribes to arms, while underground, in the kingdom of Hel, the red cockerel assembled his troops. Staying at his post, Heimdall sounded the horn on the bridge of Bilfröst: the invasion commenced. Yggdrasill, the sacred ash, was shaken by the awakening of the giants. The wolf Garm broke his chains, while, to the east, several ships full of phantoms approached the kingdom of the gods. At their head was the giant Hrym with his shield raised. At the same time, the great serpent of the world lashed boats with his coil, before tossing the fleet of dead onto the shore. Loki, who had broken his chains, suddenly appeared from the north. Accompanied by the wolf Fenrir, he commanded a cohort of giants. From the south appeared Surt, the black giant of fire who came from Muspelsheim, bearer of a burning blade that destroyed everything in its path. The situation became untenable: the mountains collapsed, flames shot up from the earth and the dwarf people was destroyed. Under attack from these terrible assailants, the gods closed ranks and squared off in the final formation.

The ultimate battle took place on the plain of Vígríd, where the fray became inextricable. Surrounded by his faithful Valkyries, Odin flung himself at Fenrir but the monster swallowed him with his enormous jaws. Vídar immediately avenged his father by seizing the wolf and plunging a long sword into its throat. Thor hurled himself at the large serpent and landed a terrible stroke of his hammer upon its head, felling the reptile which, in its death throes, still managed to spit some fatal venom at the head of the wretched Thor. Frey, the god of fertility, succumbed to the blows of the giant Surt. T_r and the wolf Garm killed each other. Heimdall and Loki abandoned themselves to a desperate fight in which both of them perished. The valiant warriors of Walhalla threw themselves into a final assault on the giants but could not avoid the inevitable. The earth burst into flames and was then swallowed up by wild floods. All, or almost all, of the gods were massacred and Ásgard disappeared in a storm. Men perished with them, for the earth, devoured by fire and invaded by the waters, became practically uninhabitable. The only survivor was Yggdrasill, the sacred ash, surrounded by total destruction. The sons of Odin and of Thor were spared by the catastrophe. A new world was able rise up from the void. Another sun rose over the virgin earth ("For a second time earth covered in vegetation suddenly appeared from the waves") and a couple of humans soon gave birth to a sturdy people. Baldr, the righteous, came back to life and prayed for this renaissance. Without denying their respective existences, men and gods reassumed the course of history. The seeress concluded her story thus: "I saw rise up a brilliant assembly like the sun; it is there where the valiant people will live, they will live in joy and peace for the time to come."

The Heroes and the Dragon Slayers

If the Nordic imagination appears particularly rich and multi-faceted, there is also a more traditional domain where Germanic mythology exercises an undeniable power of fascination, by introducing characters found in the legendary heritage of most civilisations: exceptional heroes. We are entering into the universe of the medieval epic, whose roots sometimes go back to the dawn of time.

Wolfram von Eschenbach, the author of *Parzival*

"Perceval was received with extreme courtesy; admitted to the royal table; he beheld how the feast of the Grail was repeated (...) The guests had just taken their seats when a young woman came out of a neighbouring room carrying two silver tools; after her came a valet holding up high a spear from which was dripping blood. Finally the Grail appeared, held by invisible hands. It passed twice along the tables which were immediately covered with everything that each person wanted. But Perceval did not seem to see this divine miracle." (La Queste du Saint Graal, adaptation by Albert Pauphilet, 1923) [The Quest for the Holy Grail]. In his Parzifal, Wolfram von Eschenbach took up the thread of the epic story by Chrétien de Troyes, Perceval or The Quest for the Grail.

The knight poet Wolfram von Eschenbach in the 13th century, Heidelberg.

Feudal society and Christian themes inspired a number of epic stories featuring Beowulf, Sigmund and Sigurd.

The ancient heroic songs and the Waltharius

The most ancient text written in old German is undoubtedly the *Lay of Hildebrand*, which goes back to the first part of the 9th century. It retraces the confrontation between the hero Hildebrand, spokesman of Theodoric, king of the Ostrogoths, and his own son. Rejected by his son, who thought him dead, Hildebrand, his heart broken, resolved to kill his son in the duel that was to pit them against each other. A legendary figure, who perhaps had a historical model, Hildebrand reappeared in the lay of the Nibelungs as a master of arms.

The *Waltharius*, an epic poem composed in Latin at the beginning of the 10th century, relates the great deeds of Walter, the son of the King of Aquitaine, and of his betrothed, the Burgundian Hildegrund. They manage to escape from the camp of Attila, where they were being held prisoner. Mixing themes of antique or Christian inspiration with Germanic elements, this story is a reminder of the invasion of the Huns, already described in ancient songs of Gothic origin. At a certain moment, the heroes and Gunther, chief of the Burgundians, concluded a blood pact (das blutige Bündnis). This did not, however, prevent Gunther from being killed by Attila. The legend continued to be told until the 13th century in Germany and certainly contributed to feeding the old mythical traditions of the Nibelungs.

Aside from these texts of pagan inspiration, there also exist Christian poems, which return to the origins and the end of the world: *Heiland*, written around 830 in Low German; and the *Muspilli*, composed in the 10th century in Bavarian. The poem *Ruodlieb*, written in Latin in the 11th century, introduces a knight without fear and without reproach. Although influenced by Christian sentiments (the author was a monk in Bavaria), this hero, nevertheless, shows himself to be an exceptional warrior, and an animal tamer without compare, who renders bears, wolves and other savage beasts as docile as lambs. He heralds the arrival, in German literature, of the character of *Parzifal*, created in the 13th century by Wolfram von Eschenbach, based on the *Perceval* of Chrétien de Troyes.

Following pages
The vanquished dragon
Beowulf, Sigmund the Völsung, Sigard, Siegfried, Dietrich – many heroes and dragon slayers who perpetuated the myth, an integral part of Nordic tradition.

The legend of Beowulf and Grendel

The most famous epic of ancient English literature was undoubtedly written in the 10th century. The story takes place in the 6th century and paints an interesting picture of the heroic life of the people of the North, where warrior valour and courage were exalted but justice and law too. This long poem of more than three thousand verses tells of the exploits of the hero, Beowulf, Prince of Sweden. It is a legend of German origin but its echo is found in several Scandinavian sagas. At the end of a stinking marsh, in a Danish forest, lived the terrible Grendel, a water giant with the body of a serpent who terrorised the region and even invaded the castle of King Hrodgar. Night after night he returned to haunt places, so that nowhere felt safe. The reputation of this monster was such that it soon reached the country of the Goths. A young warrior, Beowulf, decided to take up the challenge and to rid Denmark of the sinister Grendel. Accompanied by a small group of loyal troops, he decided to go to the palace of King Hrodgar and explain the mission that he had taken upon himself.

The task was not easy and many knights had already perished in the attempt; their blood covered the banks of the swamp where Grendel wreaked havoc. The combat started on the first night and Grendel nearly surprised Beowulf. In the darkest part of the night, "he who walks in the shadows" entered the chamber of the valiant hero and seized one of Beowulf's companions. Beowulf stood up and grabbed the giant. In a desperate fight, he managed to crush the assault and cut off one of the giant's legs. Mortally wounded, Grendel beat his retreat and plunged into the stagnant water of the marsh. The following morning, the dormant waters were full of blood. Grendel had been felled. The King paid homage to Odin and to the hero, the finest of the warriors. A great feast was organised and, during the feast, Beowulf was showered with sumptuous gifts: a helmet, a breastplate, a spear and a gilded banner.

The joy of the Danes was short lived. That night, a new monster appeared: the mother of Grendel, who had resolved to avenge her son. Appearing from the depths, she seized several warriors with her talons and took them into the waters of the marsh. Beowulf set off in pursuit of her, crossing inhospitable lands – winding paths, sour ponds, forests with trees of tangled branches, raging torrents – to finally arrive at the shores of a sombre sea, with fierce waves crashing.

The battle horns sounded and the troops took position. Saying his farewells to the companions who surrounded him, the hero did not hesitate for an instant before diving into the gloom. Once again there was a desperate fight and Beowulf had to confront the she-wolf of the wild sea. His coat of mail protected him from the creature's talons and he was able to reach its lair. The final confrontation took place in an underwater cavern. Seizing an immense spear, probably forged in former times by the giants, Beowulf decapitated the monster. Before returning to the surface, he found the body of Grendel and cut off its head. At the surface, the Danes were sad to see the waters tainted with blood. "It's the end!", they said, "The noble hero could not triumph over the she-wolf!" Several moments later, Beowulf appeared brandishing the head of the monster. He was celebrated accordingly and Hrodgar thanked him warmly.

The symbolism of this legend appears clearly to allude to the merging of water and rock: the giant of the waters, Grendel, represents the crash of floods and the risks of the storms threatened the shores of the North Sea.

Beowulf and the dragon

Upon returning to the kingdom of the Danes, Beowulf saw his renown grow and, acclaimed by his people, took the throne. He governed with clear-sightedness for fifty years but at the end of his reign a terrible scourge afflicted his people. A dragon, the guardian of a treasure which had been stolen from him, started to ravage the country to take revenge. Wild with anger, he set out every night and breathed fire onto the houses of the inhabitants, sowing desolation. Beowulf set off to meet the monster. Once again, he proved his extraordinary courage. This was a duel to the death with terror upon terror.

Helped by the young Wiglaf, the old king finished off the dragon but was mortally wounded during the confrontation. Beowulf perished on the floor of the cavern, covered in blood. Before he died, he spoke to his vassal Wiglaf, giving him his necklace and his ring of gold: "You are the last of our race; seeing as destiny has taken all of our parents, I am going to join them (…) Say to those who fight bravely that they should build, at the place of the funeral pyre, a very high mound on the rock which hangs over the sea. In this way, mariners and navigators may honour my memory." This was done in a poignant ceremony where the warriors paid homage to their chief.

The death of Beowulf is reminiscent of that of Thor, who, during Ragnarök, killed the great serpent of the world but succumbed to its venom.

The lay of the Nibelungs

Little by little, society changed and the feudal model triumphed. The idea of chivalry dominated the scene. As in the rest of Europe, the court narrative became established with the works of Gottfried de Strasbourg, Hartmann von Aue and Wolfram von Eschenbach, who introduced the story of the Knights of the Round Table and the myths of King Arthur and of Tristan and Isolde to their countries.

These stories were inspired by those of Chrétien de Troyes or the *Roman de Brut*, but they also add a profoundly original vision, enriching the theme. These works, collecting souvenirs from the heroic time of the Germanic lands, were conveyed by the *Minnesänger*. In the manner of the troubadours of southern France, they visited princes and lords, introducing them to their repertoire. The *Meistersänger* contested their supremacy but they addressed more the people and gave priority to less refined songs. Nevertheless, the great German heroic epic remains the story that features Siegfried, Gunther, Brunhild, Kriemhilde, Hagan and Alberich and which exalts the warrior virtues of the Germanic people.

Composed around 1200 at the court of the Bishop of Passau, the lay of the Nibelungs mixes two ancient legends, that of the Burgundians and of Siegfried, with diverse historical elements from the 3rd and 4th centuries. There are many versions of the legend including *The Lay of Volund*, a Nordic story of the Edda, where Siegfried (from old German: Seyfried) calls himself Sigurd (from ancient Nordic: Sigurdh) and takes over from his father Sigmund the Völsung. He proved himself an accomplished hero when he managed to take from an oak a magic sword, which Odin had planted there. In the first texts, Sigurd was raised by the blacksmith Regin, who initiated him in many magic practices. He had two brothers: the dragon Fáfnir, guardian of the fabulous treasure, and Otr, who sometimes assumed the appearance of an otter.

One day Loki killed the animal and, in order to avenge him, his father, Hreidmar, decided to capture Loki, Odin and Hœnir. They would only be released in return for a large quantity of gold. So Odin persuaded Loki to go and steal the treasure from the dwarf Andvari. This he managed and the gods got out of trouble. The dwarf, however, cast a spell over them and the curse of Andvari worked wonderfully: Fáfnir killed his father, Hreidmar, to take possession of the treasure; then he changed into a dragon to protect his riches.

Regin encouraged Sigurd to kill the dragon in order to take his treasure. To this end, he forged him a magic sword from the pieces of the sword of his father, Sigmund. Sigurd felled Fáfnir and roasted the heart of the dragon. While doing this, he grazed his finger. Upon bringing this finger to his mouth, Sigurd was able to understand the language of the birds and, overhearing their song, he learned that Regin was intending to kill him. Without hesitation, Sigurd cut off the head of the blacksmith and seized the treasure.

The curse of the ring continued, nevertheless, and brought about the disappearance of Sigurd ("This noisy gold, this red-fire treasure, these rings will bring you death," predicted Fáfnir to him).

Advancing ever further southwards, in the direction of Hindarfjall, Sigurd one day saw a great light at the top of the mountain. It was there that Brunhild was resting, surrounded by flames so high that they reached the sky. The young woman with long plaits of gold had been punished by Odin for her loose living. Heeding only his courage, Sigurd brought his trusty warhorse, Grani, to a gallop and jumped the circle of fire. He thus broke the spell and made the acquaintance of Brunhild.

They became lovers and swore faithfulness to each other. Sigurd rode on his way and finally arrived at the castle of King Gjúki. There he met Gunnar (Gunther in the lay of the Nibelungs) and Högni (Hagen in the lay of the Nibelungs), the sons of the king, as well as the beautiful Gúdrun.

The queen, who knew the love that Sigurd had for Brunhild, manipulated the situation in such a way that the gallant knight became the lover of her daughter Gúdrun: She invited Sigurd to a great banquet and handed him the sacred horn containing a magic brew. He took it and drank the enchanted mead. In that moment, Sigurd forgot the circle of fire and Brunhild. The queen Kriemhilde then convinced her husband Gjúki and their two sons to rally to the plan: "Sigurd is a powerful man, dressed in gold, and an exceptional hero …We should offer him our daughter!" Everything went according to her wishes and, during a magnificent feast, Sigurd married Gúdrun. Kriemhilde knew, however, that Brunhild's magic was without compare and preferred to take precautions. She went to find her son Gunnar and encouraged him to take Brunhild for his wife. So he set off, accompanied by Högni and Sigurd, having decided to ask for Brunhild's hand in marriage. Since, despite his courage, Gunnar did not manage to overcome the obstacle of fire, he changed appearance with Sigurd who agreed to pay court to Brunhild on his behalf. The task proved difficult because the Valkyrie remained faithful to Sigurd but he was so persuasive that she eventually gave in. Sigurd and Gunnar reassumed their own appearances and returned to the castle.

The marriage of Brunhild and Gunnar was celebrated several days later. Alas, one day Brunhild recognised, on the finger of Gúdrun, the ring of gold that Sigurd had given her in former times, and she immediately understood her mistake. Full of bitterness, she severely reprimanded Gunther and showed Sigurd up to be a liar. From that day forward, she had only one thing on her mind: to avenge herself and cause the demise of her former betrothed. When Sigurd was stabbed at her instigation, Brunhild, in tears, took a sword and ran herself through. She then turned to Gunther and addressed him: "I ask you for a final favour. On the funeral pyre that you will build, please reserve a place for me next to Sigurd ..." Then she fell silent. When the flames rose up from the funeral pyre where Sigurd had been laid, Brunhild threw herself into the inferno. So it was that the two lovers in death kept the oath which they had not respected in life.

In the epic of the Nibelungs, Siegfried, descended from the prestigious family of the Völsung, destroyed a famous dragon and bathed in the blood of the monster. On account of this, his skin became as hard as horn, rendering him invulnerable, except for one point on his back between the shoulder blades, where a leaf had fallen from a tree; the place at which Hagen hurled a fatal javelin. Siegfried then got rid of the kings of the Nibelungs and came into possession of their fabulous treasure, keeping the magic ring. Because of this, the hero fell under the curse and got caught up in the fatal circumstances evoked by the King Eugel: "Power engenders arrogance. The sound of gold and the sparkle of diamonds wake in man bad spirits and he can only be good as long as these spirits sleep. One example serves as a warning. This treasure has already brought about more than one crime." (Raupach) Protected by his sword Balmung, Siegfried received, from the dwarf Alberich, a helmet that made him invisible. He then freed Brunhild from the curse of Wotan and set off for the kingdom of the Burgundians, where his exploits enabled him to win over Kriemhilt, the sister of King Gunther.

After the marriage of Brunhild and Gunther, the Burgundian lord, Hagen, promised to avenge the offence that Siegfried had committed against her and killed the hero. Seizing the treasure, Hagen became Kriemhilt's bête noire and she vowed to kill him. Invited to the court of King Etzel (Attila), he defied the Huns and Kriemhilt before perishing in the tournament. During the general conflagration, Kriemhilt cut off Hagen's head with Siegfried's sword.

In the 16th century, the legendary theme was adapted for stage by Hans Sachs but fell, little by little, into obscurity. At the beginning of the 19th century, von den Hagen translated the poem and made it accessible to larger numbers of people, attracting the praise of Goethe. After the *Nibelungen* (1861) by Hebel, who merged different versions, Richard Wagner, with *The Ring* (*The Rhine Gold* 1868; *The Valkyrie* 1879; *Siegfried*, 1876; *The Twilight of the Gods*, 1876), conceived a magnificent work and gave the legend back its purity. Identifying Siegfried as a sun deity, he made the treasure the central element of the myth, the stakes in the fight between the forces of light and darkness. The cycle opens with the theft of the Rhine Gold by the dwarf Alberich, who forges the all-powerful ring, and ends with the conflagration of the funeral pyre of Siegfried upon which Brunhild throws herself.

In 1924, the film maker Fritz Lang made the Nibelungen, based on a screenplay by Théa von Harbou. He explains his intentions: "I tried to show four different universes. Firstly, the primitive forest in which live the deformed Mim, who teaches Siegfried to forge his sword, the dragon, and the subterranean kingdom of Alberich, dwarf guardian of the treasure of the Nibelungs, which he curses when he is beaten by Siegfried. Secondly, the castle enveloped in flames of the Amazon queen of Iceland, Brunhild. Thirdly, the stylised world, slightly degenerated, highly civilised, of the Kingdom of the Burgundians, on the point of disintegration. And finally, the world

of the wild Asian hordes of the Huns and their clash with the world of the Burgundians." (Lotte Eisner, *Fritz Lang*).

The revival of Romanticism

Rare are the peoples, who, like the Germans, have conserved the recollection of their myths and legends within their collective memory. The rediscovery of these has undoubtedly played a very important role.

Charles Perrault, as early as the end of the 17th century, published the *Contes de ma mere l'Oye*. In Germany itself, Herder, Wieland and Goethe were interested in these tales but without, however, giving them the national dimension, which they would acquire through Romanticism. At the end of the 18th century, the reaction of the *Sturm und Drang*, and in the 19th century, the Romantic movement, which formed against the rationalism of the Enlightenment, encouraged a growing German interest in their roots. If the first wave of Romanticism, that of the Iena school, which comprised the brothers Schlegel, Ludwig Tieck, Jean-Paul, Hölderlin and Novalis, leaned towards a universal idealism inspired by Friedrich Wilhelm Schelling (the author of the German *System of Idealism*, 1800), a new Romanticism, marked by the Napoleonic occupation, was born in the parlours of Heidelberg, Dresden and Berlin. Tieck had discovered the magic of the Middle Ages and revived it with the memory of an idealised Germany. Novalis, author of Hymns to the Night and Spiritual Songs, pledged his allegiance to Frederick Barbarossa, when his hero, Heinrich von Ofterdingen, came to visit the noble old man in his mountain in Thuringia. Universalism soon gave up its place to the cult of tradition and the nation rediscovered. The second Romanticism, of which the principal representatives are Achim von Arnim, Joseph von Eichendorff, Clemens Brentano, the Brothers Grimm, Chamisso and Hoffmann, rejected reason and proposed rediscovering the great collective intuitions expressed markedly in popular fairy tales (*Märchen*). Tieck wrote the Völksmärchen, Joseph von Görres also leaned towards popular tradition and was at the head of the nationalist movement, resisting the armies of Napoleon. The theoretician of Germanness (*Deutschheit*), which is also expressed in the powerful texts of the philosopher Adam Müller, is Johann Gottlieb Fichte, whose *Addresses to the German Nation* appeared in 1808.

"All the *Märchen* are only dreams of this familiar world which is everywhere and nowhere." This phrase from Novalis enables us to understand the passion felt by the Romantics in researching their roots. Arnim and Brentano published *The Boy's Magic Horn* (1806 – 1808) which brings together more than seven hundred songs and texts; Görres wrote an anthology of tales and German legends (*Deutsche Volksbücher*, 1807); Jakob Grimm, philologist and author of numerous works, including *German Mythology*, wrote, with his brother Wilhelm, a collection of tales (1829), the fruit of incessant research work over several years. Later, the Brothers Grimm edited *German Legends*, which included many myths such as those of Frederick Barbarossa, Lohengrin, Till Eulenspiegel and Tannhäuser. Besides such traditional tales as *Little Red Riding Hood*, *Puss in Boots* and *Blue Beard*, already presented by Perrault, the entire universe of *Volkslieder* and *Volksmärchen* was reborn thanks to these writers, who saved these little joys of literature from obscurity: *Snow White*, *Mother Holle*, *Hansel and Gretel*, *The Pied Piper of Hamlin* and *The Mouse Tower Bingen*. This rediscovery of forgotten heritage evokes the waking dream of Ludwig Tieck:

"At the end of memory, of the unfathomable depths of the past, an unknown power suddenly brought forth all the figures, which formerly filled it with joy and terror; rudely awakened, all these uncertain phantoms reappeared, without a precise form, flying through the air and often surrounding our heads with a wild buzzing." (*les Amis*).

One dreams of the *Aurelia* of Nerval or of certain pages of Victor Hugo, striding over the mountain ruins of the Rhineland: "All the monsters of the shadow rise and start to teem. The bat flaps its wings, the spider bangs the wall with its hammer. The toad makes it hideous rasp. I know not which venomous, gloomy life crawls between the stones, the grass, the branches. And then, the deaf roars, strange knockings, glares, crackling under the leaves, faint sighs heard all around you, unknown moaning, different beings exhale doleful sounds, that which is never heard howled or murmured, for you never see, chambers demolished and deserted; these are the screech owls, who moan like the dying." (*The Rhine*).

The Ballad of Lenora where the dead go quickly

Germanism and supernatural Romanticism, on the fringes of The Ballad of Lenora *(1770), by the German poet Gottfried August Bürger. Believing that she has found her betrothed, Lenora rides with a mysterious knight who is none other than Death herself. The terrible ride takes them to the tomb where the betrothed is located but all that remains is his armour and his skeleton.*

The Ballad of Lenora, 1839,
Horace Vernet
Musée de Beaux Arts, Nantes.

Following pages
Heidelberg: The house of the Knight of Saint George

"It was the hour where the facades of the old abandoned edifices are no longer facades but faces. I walked forward on the hilly and uneven cobbles without daring to make any noise and I experienced within the four walls of this enclosure this strange discomfort, this indefinable feeling which the ancients called the horror of the sacred forests. There is a sort of insurmountable terror in the catastrophe mixed with the superb."
Victor Hugo, The Rhine, 1842).

Drawing by Victor Hugo.

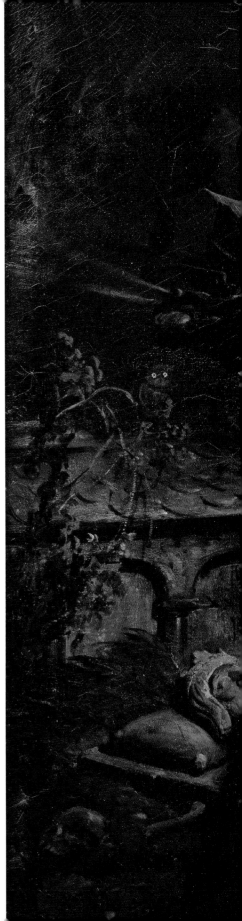